Man of fifty-five or sixty. Height: 5'6". Osteoarthritis, scoliosis, and arterial atheroma. Bandages perfectly preserved.

Robust man of forty or forty-five. Height: 5'8". Probable cause of death: Bilharzia. Major part of bandages preserved.

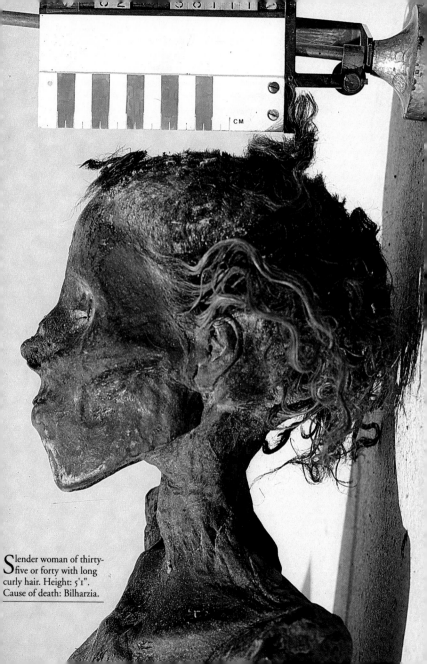

Slender woman of thirty-five or forty with long curly hair. Height: 5'1". Cause of death: Bilharzia.

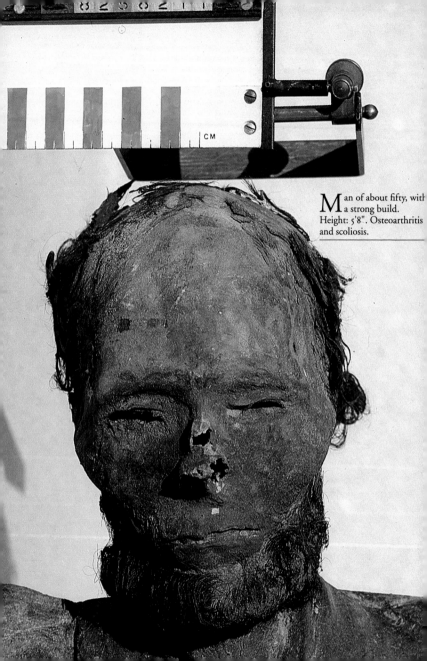

Man of about fifty, with a strong build. Height: 5'8". Osteoarthritis and scoliosis.

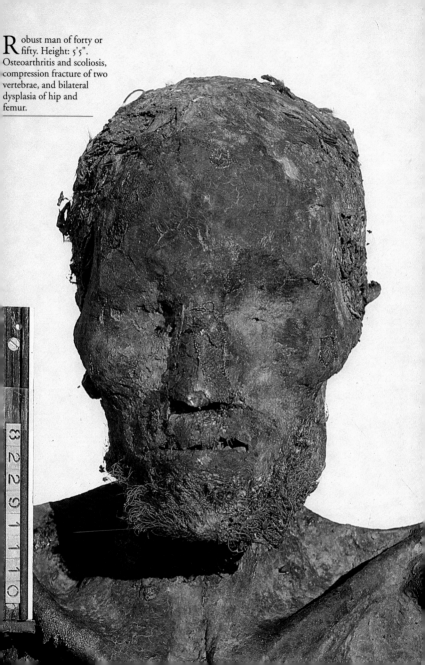

Robust man of forty or fifty. Height: 5'5". Osteoarthritis and scoliosis, compression fracture of two vertebrae, and bilateral dysplasia of hip and femur.

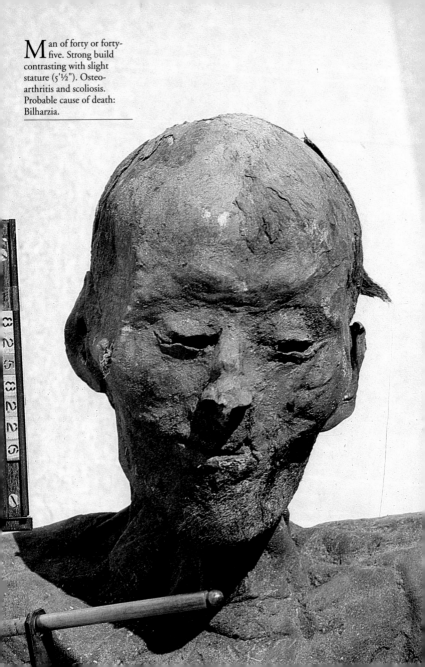

Man of forty or forty-five. Strong build contrasting with slight stature (5'½"). Osteo-arthritis and scoliosis. Probable cause of death: Bilharzia.

Woman of about sixty. Height: 5'3". Decalcified bones and poor dental condition, advanced osteo-arthritis, and a prolapsed womb.

CM

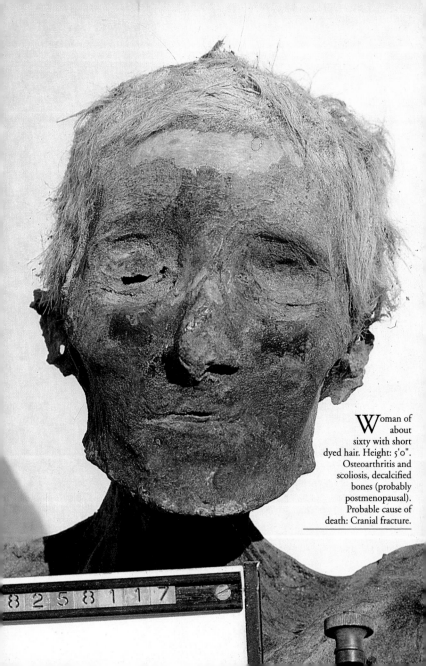

Woman of about sixty with short dyed hair. Height: 5'0". Osteoarthritis and scoliosis, decalcified bones (probably postmenopausal). Probable cause of death: Cranial fracture.

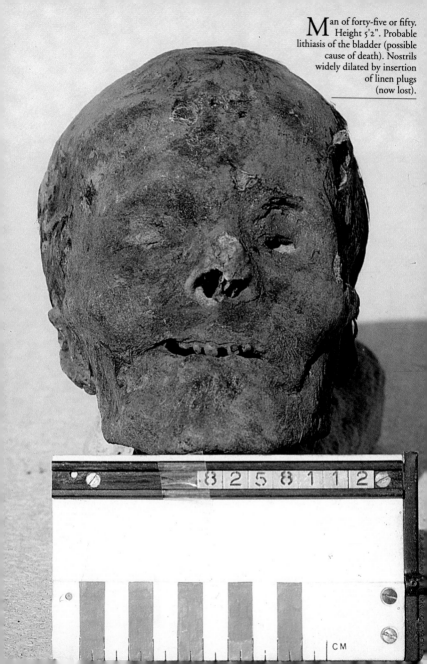

Man of forty-five or fifty. Height 5'2". Probable lithiasis of the bladder (possible cause of death). Nostrils widely dilated by insertion of linen plugs (now lost).

CONTENTS

MUMMIES
A VOYAGE THROUGH ETERNITY

Françoise Dunand and Roger Lichtenberg

DISCOVERIES

HARRY N. ABRAMS, INC., PUBLISHERS

Travelers of antiquity marveled at Egypt. The Greek historian Herodotus, writing in the 5th century BC, said that the inhabitants of this strange country "did everything differently from everyone else." While the Greeks cremated their dead, the Egyptians attempted to preserve in theirs the semblance of life. Because of such writings, in the West, Egypt has always been thought of as the land of mummies.

CHAPTER I

MUMMIES COME TO LIGHT

The 17th-century image of mummies was still fanciful (opposite). Giovanni Battista Belzoni's lithograph of the Great Chamber in the second pyramid at Giza (1818) is a more accurate record.

Mummies were among the many wonders discovered by the first Europeans to venture along the banks of the Nile in the 15th century.

It Quickly Became Fashionable for Travelers to Take Back Souvenirs: Statues, Amulets, and Even Coffins, Complete with Their Occupants

In 1605 a Frenchman named Du Castel bought a mummy and two sarcophagi in Cairo. Several decades later the poet Jean de La Fontaine, seeing them in the home of Nicolas Fouquet, the wealthy financier and patron of the arts, was prompted to write: "The coffins or tombs of King Chephren and King Cheops have been shipped here recently (not without effort and expense) in great haste from a strange land." (A completely fanciful identification, we should add.) The painter Peter Paul Rubens also owned one, which he used as a model for a number of drawings.

Starting in the 16th century, powdered mummy, known as *mumiya*, was regarded as a panacea and was found on apothecaries' shelves. Trading in mummy became a lucrative business and inevitably led to the manufacture of false *mumiya* to meet growing demand.

Two major events marked the beginnings of Egyptology, the scientific study of ancient Egypt. In 1798 Napoleon Bonaparte assembled an army and invaded Egypt. The military operation itself was a fiasco, but Napoleon had the brilliant idea of taking with him a group of experts whose job it was to produce an exhaustive inventory of the country's monuments, flora, and fauna. The result was the massive *Description of Egypt*, published between 1809 and 1822.

In 1822, in a letter dated 27 September to the permanent secretary of the Académie des Inscriptions et Belles-Lettres in Paris, the young scholar Jean-François Champollion (1790–1832)—who had not taken part in Napoleon's expedition—announced that he had

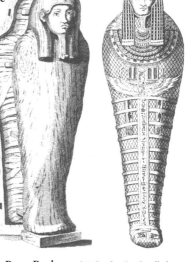

The first book called *Description of Egypt* (1735) was based on the memoirs of Benoît de Maillet, French consul in Egypt (1692–1708). The illustrations above, which are taken from it (left: an open coffin revealing the bandaged mummy; right: a cartonnage, the casing for a mummy) are fairly accurate.

The pyramids and sphinx at Giza (opposite above) in a 1657 book, are much more schematic. The sphinx, whose head alone was visible above the sand, is labeled Ablehon, a distortion of its Arab name, Abu el Hul, meaning "the father of terror."

succeeded in deciphering Egyptian hieroglyphs. Thanks to this major linguistic breakthrough, the land of the pharaohs was to emerge from fifteen centuries of silence.

Europe in the Grip of Egyptomania

Motifs inspired by ancient Egypt invaded the decorative arts, architecture, and interior furnishings. Collections, both public and private, were enriched with a wealth of Egyptian artifacts. To meet the growing demand, pillaging of ancient sites increased, and mummies and sarcophagi were regularly shipped over to Europe. Not all survived the journey: The sarcophagus belonging to the 4th-dynasty pharaoh Mykerinus, for example, went down with the ship that was carrying it to England and now lies somewhere in the Mediterranean. Many Egyptian antiquities ended up in museums as donations by private collectors. Though only a tiny minority of

A Napoleonic soldier supervising the transport of a mummy (below), a detail from an early-19th-century painting by Léon Cogniet. The painting is in the Louvre, on the ceiling of a room designed to house Champollion's Egyptian collection.

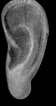

Egypt Discovered

On 19 May 1798 10,000 sailors and 36,000 soldiers set sail from France for Egypt. With them was a team of mathematicians, astronomers, engineers, naturalists, artists, and printers armed with Arabic, Greek, and Latin characters. For two years they studied everything from the quality of Nile water to mirages and the possibility of linking the Red Sea with the Mediterranean (the future Suez Canal). Their principal interest, however, was Egypt's past. The result was the massive *Description of Egypt*, from which the watercolors on this page are taken. Above: A human ear, probably part of a funerary mask; left: funerary statuettes known as ushabtis. The hieroglyphs were perfectly reproduced in the watercolors, although no one could decipher them at the time.

The members of the expedition at work, as depicted by Léon Cogniet (opposite).

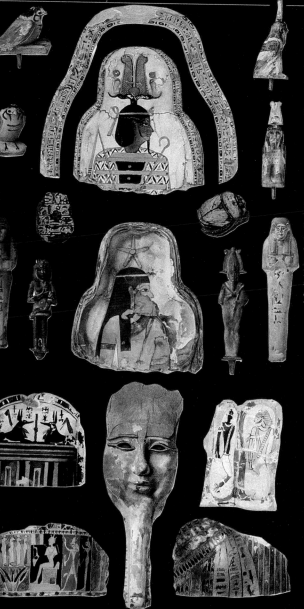

The Richest Museum in the World

The *Description of Egypt* was designed to be an exhaustive study. Along with depicting the ancient monuments and antiquities (illustrated here), it aimed also to provide an inventory of contemporary flora and fauna (scientific research overlapped with economic interest) and a systematic survey of ethnographic and geographic features. The work, in nine volumes of text and eleven volumes of illustrations, comprising 907 color plates and more than 3000 illustrations, took almost twenty years to complete.

mummies was shipped abroad, those that did remain in Egypt were not safe from pilfering hands. Looters in search of jewels and amulets overlooked by their ancient predecessors had no scruples about stripping their victims or even tearing them to pieces. Animal remains were also plundered: Throughout the 19th century England alone imported hundreds of tons of mummified cat for the sole purpose of manufacturing fertilizer.

Mummies were initially regarded as no more than objects of curiosity, but over time interest assumed a more scientific slant. During the 19th century meetings were organized to mark the ceremonial unwrapping of mummies. Often the only point was to collect some item of value, but, as if to give the operation scientific credibility, a brief description was sometimes drawn up.

In 1908 Margaret Murray (wearing an apron), of the University of Manchester, conducted a clinical investigation of an adult male mummy dating to the 12th dynasty (c. 1991–1786 BC). The mummy was discovered in the course of official excavations carried out by the great English archaeologist Sir William Flinders Petrie (1852–1942) in Lower Egypt. After 1858 no sites could be excavated or antiquities exported without the permission of the Antiquities Service in Cairo.

"When I See, and Touch, the Bodies of So Many Illustrious Persons We Never Imagined Could Be More Than Names to Us,...I Still Find It Hard to Believe That I Am Not Dreaming"

"Where I had expected to meet one or two petty kings," continued Gaston Maspero (1846–1916), director of the Egyptian Antiquities Service, "the Arabs had uncovered a whole vault full of kings. And what kings!" Packed in together in a cache at Deir el-Bahari, Maspero had discovered the most famous pharaohs of the New Kingdom (1550–1085 BC): Amosis I, Tuthmosis I, II, and III, Amenophis I, Ramses II and III, and Seti I, along with their queens—Nefertari and Aahotep among them—and numerous princes and princesses, as well as major court officials. This fabulous discovery was made as a result of a cross between a police investigation and an Eastern fairy tale.

The appearance of royal burial goods on the antiquities market during the previous decade or so had attracted archaeological attention.

Maspero began making inquiries in Luxor, and these eventually led him to a family living in the village of Gourna, near the Valley of the Kings: the three Abd el-Rassul brothers. One finally admitted that the three had been dealing in stolen burial goods, and on 5 July 1881 he revealed the whereabouts of the cache, at the end of a shaft opening high up on a rock face.

L uigi Mayer's depiction of Egyptian antiquities in the hallway of a country house in Bulaq (above), in *Views in Egypt* (1801–4). Below: The mummy of Ramses II.

Maspero and his fellow archaeologists realized that the former masters of Egypt could not be treated in the same way as their obscure subjects, and the entire contents of the Deir el-Bahari cache were transported by river to the museum at Bulaq, in the suburbs of Cairo. On both banks of the Nile, Maspero wrote, "disheveled peasant women followed the boat howling like animals, and the men fired shots in the way that they do at a funeral." In Cairo the archaeologists had to pay duty on the mummies, which were classified as, of all things, dried fish.

In 1898 French Archaeologist Victor Loret (1859–1946) Found the Tomb of Amenophis II in the Valley of the Kings, on the West Bank of the Nile. The Pharaoh Was Still in His Coffin

This was the first time that a royal tomb had been found complete with its occupant. Buried with the pharaoh was his bow, which he alone was entitled to draw. The mummies of eight other pharaohs from the New Kingdom were discovered in a side chamber of the tomb. These were taken to Cairo; Amenophis (ruled 1421–1401 BC) remained where he was. His peace was short-lived, however. Word soon got out that there were still treasures in the tomb, and, despite the presence of an armed guard, it was looted and the pharaoh's body was torn to pieces. From the ensuing inquiry it appeared that the guards themselves may have had some hand in the affair.

The archaeological exploration of tombs and burial sites gradually became more regular and systematic. At the beginning of the 20th century, the large burial

Howard Carter opening one of the four gilded wood shrines, the innermost of which housed the sarcophagus containing the wooden coffins of Tutankhamun (above).

Opposite: A bust of Tutankhamun found in the antechamber to his tomb. The figure, which is made of wood covered with painted plaster, has a fairly lifelike expression and wears the headdress associated with the god Amun. The function it served is not known.

The funerary mask of Prince Khaemuset, from the time of Ramses II, found at Saqqara (left).

chambers at Abydos, in the Valley of the Kings, at Saqqara, and in Nubia were all excavated, as were many less important sites. These excavations brought to light abundant artifacts and human or animal remains.

At around this time the first anthropological studies were undertaken, primarily on skeletons. X-raying, used on mummies from 1896 onward, failed to produce any significant results until the 1930s. Unfortunately, unless they belonged to kings or important court officials, mummies were still not always studied with the attention they deserved.

For Years the Young English Artist and Egyptologist Howard Carter (1874–1939) Explored the Valley of the Kings, Convinced That There Were Still Secrets to Be Uncovered

On 26 November 1922 Carter entered the virtually intact tomb of Tutankhamun, an obscure pharaoh of the end of the 18th dynasty. It was the first time that an archaeologist had discovered a royal tomb with almost all its burial goods in place. The goods were for the most part of the highest quality, and it would take six years to remove them all from the chamber. Given the astonishing wealth lavished on a young king who reigned briefly during a period of great political upheaval, we can only guess what riches the tomb of a king as powerful as Ramses II might have contained.

"A Marvelous Journey Worthy of the Thousand and One Nights"

On 17 March 1939, after a decade of excavation at Tanis, French archaeologist Pierre Montet

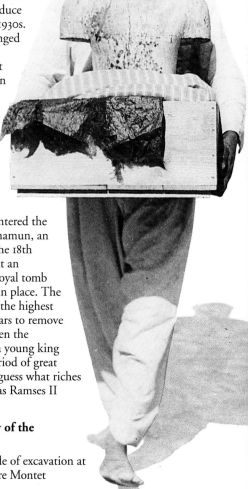

(1885–1966) discovered the tomb of Sheshonq I, a pharaoh from the 22nd dynasty, the Shishak of the Bible. Tanis, a vast site in the eastern Nile delta, had been a city of great importance at the end of the New Kingdom. Sheshonq's burial chamber was situated within the precinct of the temple of Amun.

The sarcophagi and funerary goods of a number of other pharaohs were subsequently uncovered, notably those of Psousennes I (21st dynasty, 1085–945 BC). The Tanis excavations were certainly as important as the discovery of Tutankhamun's tomb, but the significance of the find was obscured by the outbreak of the Second World War a few months later.

The Tanis tombs were the last royal tombs to be uncovered. Some three hundred kings ruled Egypt, but many of their tombs have never been found: Only about twenty-five burial chambers and a few dozen pyramids have been uncovered. Moreover, very few royal mummies have survived intact.

Other Discoveries, Though Less Spectacular, Have Provided Egyptologists with a Mine of Information

Excavations of other burial sites have continued under the auspices of the Egyptian Antiquities Service and a number of foreign archaeological missions. At Saqqara, a

A pectoral ornament belonging to Sheshonq II depicts a scarab, symbol of rebirth (above left). Left: A gold plaque used to conceal the abdominal opening through which Psousennes's vital organs were removed. Opposite below: The same pharaoh's gold sandals. All these objects, found at Tanis, were clearly designed for ceremonial purposes.

large site (of about sixty square miles) known to house a number of very ancient tombs as well as some much later ones, recent excavations have uncovered tombs belonging to court officials of the New Kingdom period. Much more modest sites from a range of periods are currently being excavated in the Theban region (the Valley of the Queens), the oases of the western desert (Duch, Balat, and Muzawaga), Middle Egypt (Antinoë), the Fayuum, and the Nile delta, and many mummies have been uncovered in the course of these excavations.

Numerous teams of botanists, anthropologists, and radiologists provide back-up research at many sites. Thanks to their combined efforts, it has been possible to produce much more systematic population studies.

These mummies, still wrapped in their bandages (above), were excavated from the Greco-Roman necropolis at Antinoë early in this century. These excavations were carried out in a random fashion, the mummies being removed to different locations and in some cases destroyed. As a result no systematic overview was ever undertaken.

The practice of mummification dates back to the early third millennium BC, but it was not until around 1000 BC that the technique was perfected. It took centuries of experimentation, and repeated failures, for the ancient Egyptians to master the complex art of preserving in their dead the appearance of the living.

CHAPTER II
MAKING A BETTER MUMMY

A detail from the Hildesheim sarcophagus (600–300 BC) contains a rare depiction of the mummification process (opposite). In Predynastic Egypt (before about 3100 BC), bodies were buried either in the sand or in a pot, as at right.

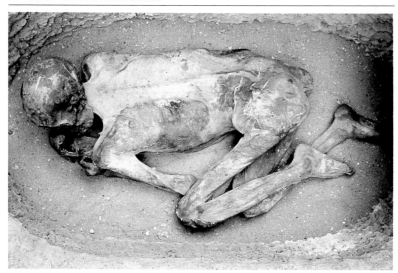

Before about 3100 BC, during the Predynastic period, prior to the unification of Upper and Lower Egypt, the dead were buried in simple graves dug in the desert sands. The sand desiccated and therefore preserved a body buried in it. The desire to afford better protection for the dead, however, coupled with technological advances, led to the construction of more elaborate tombs in the course of the 1st dynasty (starting around 3100 BC).

The protection of the body was not the only consideration. At least for kings and major court officials, funerary rites came into play. An important tomb required a chapel, where offerings could be left; it also necessitated chambers for housing the burial goods. In this type of tomb, known as a mastaba, the body was placed in a chamber at the bottom of a shaft. In the simpler style of tomb, the body was buried in a wooden or basketwork coffin inside a walled grave. In either case, deprived of the preservative effect of the sand, the body soon rotted—the very improvements intended to contribute to its preservation produced, in fact, the opposite effect. A different solution had to be found.

This mummy, known as "Ginger," is of a man who died in c. 3200 BC. It was found at Gebelein, in the desert. Ginger, who is now conserved in the British Museum in London, is a good example of natural mummification. The discovery of bodies preserved in the sand may have inspired in the ancient Egyptians the idea of life after death and led them to devise techniques for preserving the body. From this period on they placed vessels containing offerings and everyday objects near their dead.

The First Tentative Experiments

One idea was to wrap the body in cloth in order to protect it from the atmosphere. Coating the cloth in resin—so that it would stiffen and hold the body's original shape—also enhanced the preservative effect.

At the end of the 3rd dynasty (around 2575 BC), the embalmers began removing the body's abdominal organs—a fact that is indirectly confirmed by the appearance of Canopic jars, the stone vessels designed to hold these organs. They also discovered the dehydrating effect of natron, a naturally occurring compound of sodium carbonate and sodium chloride, on human and animal tissue. The viscera of Queen Hetepheres, the wife of Snefru, first king of the 4th dynasty and father of Cheops, have been found coated in natron in an alabaster box divided into four compartments.

Results, nevertheless, remain unimpressive for mummies from the Old Kingdom (3rd–6th dynasties). The bandaging process, on the other hand, became fairly sophisticated, with bandages being arranged to imitate the hang of everyday clothes. The person's facial features were painted on the shroud, and in certain cases a further refinement was introduced by coating the cloth with a layer of plaster, to preserve the angles and curves of the body (a technique that was soon abandoned).

Canopic jars with the human remains they contained (above). Champollion, who discovered the use of Canopic jars, noted: "Fibrous tissue…Animal smell/Object impregnated and covered in a thick layer of balm/Found at the bottom of the vase/Just wrapped in cloth…/Liver and brain or cerebellum." Below: A mummy in the Egyptian Museum, Turin.

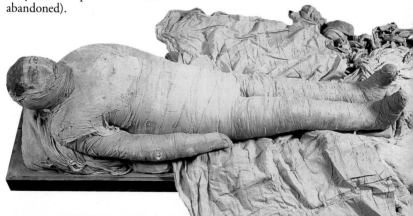

Dehydration Using Natron and Removal of the Abdominal Organs Gradually Became Widespread

Both the desiccation of the body and the removal of internal organs appear to have been common during the Middle Kingdom (2040–1786 BC), and results improved. Numerous mummies from this period have survived intact. That of Wah, an official under Mentuhotep III (11th dynasty), was wrapped in a vast quantity of material—450 square yards in total. Where inexpensive preparations were required, the embalmers made do with sand—the treatment almost certainly reserved for Mentuhotep's soldiers, whose bodies were discovered at Deir el-Bahari.

The oldest known embalming

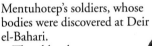

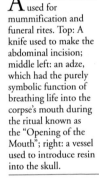

Above: Instruments used for mummification and funeral rites. Top: A knife used to make the abdominal incision; middle left: an adze, which had the purely symbolic function of breathing life into the corpse's mouth during the ritual known as the "Opening of the Mouth"; right: a vessel used to introduce resin into the skull.

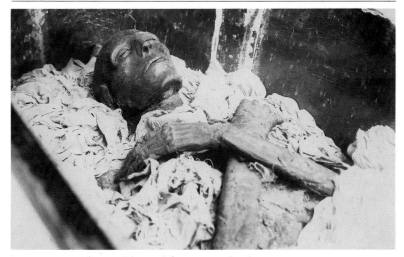

instruments and materials, used for a person by the name of Ipy, date from this period. It appears that any by-products of the embalming process were placed near the body, since they were thought to contain fragments of the deceased person.

Important advances were made during the New Kingdom with the arrival in 1550 BC of the 18th dynasty, and numerous mummies have survived from that period, many of them in very good condition. Much of what we know about mummification today comes from the study of royal mummies, which invariably received particularly careful treatment.

Embalming "According to the Best of Ways"

Herodotus wrote his nine-volume *History*, a narrative account of the wars between Greece and Persia, more than 2400 years ago. Richly detailed, it contains much incidental information gathered in the course of the

Seti I (ruled 1306–1290 BC) as found in his tomb at Deir el-Bahari, his arms crossed over his chest "Osiris" fashion (above). His mummy is extremely well preserved and is a testimony to the embalming skills of the New Kingdom. This storage box for Canopic jars (opposite below) dates from the same period and is decorated with a statue of Anubis, the jackal-headed god who led the dead to judgment, and scenes of the dead person at prayer. Canopic jars were placed under the protection of the four sons of Horus, seen here on the lids of four Canopic jars. They are (left to right): Imsety, Hapy, Duamutef, and Qebehsenuef, guardians of the liver, lungs, stomach, and intestines.

author's travels, including an essentially accurate description of the mummification process (as confirmed by modern experts). Further details are found in the account of Diodorus Siculus, a Greek traveler writing in the mid-1st century BC.

Two or three days after a person died, the body was delivered to the embalmers, who immediately extracted the viscera through an incision made below the left ribs; they removed the liver, stomach, intestines, and finally the lungs. Since the heart was regarded as the seat of consciousness and feeling (equivalent to the brain today), it was therefore essential that it not be separated from the body, and was generally left in place. The kidneys, spleen, bladder, and female reproductive organs did not receive any special treatment on the whole.

The removal of the brain was a New Kingdom innovation. Using a bronze rod inserted into the left nostril, the embalmer smashed the ethmoid bone (located at the root of the nose and separating it from the cranium) and removed the brain through the opening. Resin was then generally injected into the cranial cavity, and the resin (the precise composition of which is not known) solidified on contact with the skull. Alternatively, sawdust or cloth was packed in.

The body was sewn up again, cleaned, and then covered in natron in order to dehydrate it. The natron was applied in solid form, rather than in solution, as the term "natron bath" is often taken to imply. According to Herodotus, this operation required no less than seventy days, although this seems in fact to have been the time needed for the entire mummification process. The body was next washed in Nile water and anointed with various unguents to make it smooth and "sweet smelling." Finally, it was laid on a funeral bed in the shape of a lion, prior to being dressed.

A 19th-century engraving (above) of a late mummy (the inscription is in Greek). The incision is clearly visible, as it is in the earlier mummy below as well.

LUNIOCLATIPOCKOPNHAIOTTOAAIOT
LLLUNIOTETUNEIKOGENOCMHNUN
ETEAETTCEUL TMANOTTOTKTIOTTIATNIH

This anthropoid coffin of richly decorated wood (below) belonged to a priestess living in the 21st dynasty. Her name and religious status are inscribed on the lid. Her mummy, carefully shrouded and bandaged, was still in place when the coffin was found. The stereotypical features painted on the mask are not intended as a portrait.

"Here Come Plants Sprung from the Earth, Flax, and Restoratives. They Come to You in the Form of a Precious Shroud; They Preserve You in the Form of Bandages; They Make You Grow Larger in the Form of Linen" (Embalming Ritual)

The bandaging process was governed by a strict ritual specified in sacred books. At each step the officiating priest recited ritual formulas drawn from the texts.

The process began with the fingers, which were bandaged individually. Then came the limbs, which were also bandaged separately before being wrapped in large shrouds held in place by broader strips of cloth. The arms either rested alongside the body or were crossed over the chest in what was known as the "Osiris" pose. The head came last.

The cloth was sometimes daubed with resin, and amulets were placed between the various layers. As many as 143 amulets and other small objects were found on the mummy of Tutankhamun, and even as late as the Greco-Roman period (332 BC–AD 395) the mummy of an ordinary man or woman still concealed forty or so.

The body, now fully protected, was then placed in a coffin and returned to the family of the deceased in readiness for the funeral rites.

The *Book of the Dead* reads: "Hail, Father Osiris! I shall possess my body for ever; I shall not be corrupted; I shall not disintegrate; nor will I fall prey to worms. I exist. I am alive. I am strong. I have awoken and am at peace. There is no destruction in my organs, or in my eyes; my head has not been removed from my neck…my body is permanent; it will not perish; it will not be destroyed in this eternal land."

The mummy of a baby (above), found in its mother's coffin, has several strings of glass beads, either for decoration or for protection.

Left: Amulets were often placed in the wrappings for protection. The *djed* pillar (second from the left) was a symbol of stability; the *ankh*, or looped cross (second from the right), gave the breath of life; and the *udjat* eye (center top) had protective powers.

"For Those Who Desire the Middle Way and Wish to Avoid Great Cost"

The processes described above were very expensive, but according to Herodotus there existed two other methods of embalming that were quicker and therefore cost less. The first involved injecting an oil into the anus to dissolve the viscera prior to coating the body in natron. In the other, and cheapest, method, the body was simply washed and then desiccated using natron. Mummies in this category have upon examination revealed remnants of the viscera in various stages of decomposition.

The bandaging technique might also vary. In some cases the fingers were not bandaged separately, and the cloth, which represented the biggest expense, might be of inferior quality, or recycled household linen, instead of being specially made, as it was for first-rate embalming.

This badly damaged mummy (above), found at Antinoë, was claimed by its excavator to be that of Thaïs, the heroine of a novel by Anatole France (1844–1924). Thaïs was a prostitute in Alexandria who was converted by the monk she set out to seduce and ended her days as a penitent in the desert.

During the 21st Dynasty (1085–945 BC), Attempts Were Made to Improve Presentation

Clay, sawdust, or pads of cloth were inserted under the skin in order to enhance the contours of face and body. Artificial eyes made of glass or wood, or linen pads, were sometimes placed in the eye sockets. These attempts met with varying degrees of success, and some mummies still

In a scene from the Ani papyrus (19th dynasty, below), the dead person, in the company of his wife and relatives, is carried to his resting place on a sleigh drawn by oxen.

display the unfortunate results of being overstuffed.

Mummification became a widespread practice after about 1000 BC, which led to an increasing simplification of technique. The practice of mummification persisted after the arrival of the Greeks (332 BC) and, later, the Romans (after 30 BC) and was even adopted by many foreigners living in Egypt. The work was often still of very high quality, though it is true that numerous later mummies are poorly preserved—a reflection of sloppy workmanship and probably also constraints on costs. Some are just bags of bones, with limbs dislocated and supported with palm branches. In other cases limbs have disappeared altogether. And yet other mummies from this period demonstrate the most careful attention to detail, with an emphasis on elaborate bandaging techniques involving geometric designs and plaster decorations. It seems that at this time more effort went into the bandaging than the embalming process. Also in the Greco-Roman period, the funeral mask was replaced by a portrait painted on a wooden panel, which was then inserted into the wrappings.

Christian Mummies

The spread of Christianity in Egypt in the 3rd and especially the 4th

In Greco-Roman Egypt the funeral mask was replaced by a portrait painted on wood (left). Some of the more elaborate mummies have leaves of electrum (an alloy of gold and silver) applied to their skin. The "gilding" of the face (as above) or the limbs conferred a divine character on the recipient, since gold was regarded as the "flesh of the gods." Highly elaborate wrapping techniques, especially involving diamond patterns (left), were adopted for the wealthy. Often a painted shroud, as in the case of this one for a child (opposite left), replaced both sarcophagus and cartonnage. The "embroideress of Antinoë" (opposite right) was not bandaged at all, but simply wrapped in patterned tunics and shawls—a custom that broke with pharaonic tradition.

century AD did not put a stop to mummification. There is no evidence of any church prohibition and, indeed, the preservation of the body might well be regarded as compatible with the Christian belief in resurrection.

The few Christian mummies that have been studied reveal only minor variations from the classical treatment. For example, it became customary to bury the dead in everyday clothes or in ceremonial vestments rather than wrapping the corpse in bandages.

The Pure Place

The first mummies were treated in a tent or some other light structure near the

necropolis that housed the embalming table on which the mummy was disemboweled. After about 700 BC, as more and more mummies required treatment, these temporary workshops were replaced by permanent ones made of brick, which were often quite large. The ancient Egyptians called the embalming house *wabt*, the Pure Place, or *per nefer*, the Beautiful House—a reminder that the object of mummification was to purify and deify the dead person, regarded as an incarnation of Osiris, the god of the underworld.

The embalmers were organized into a strict hierarchy. The most important positions were the Controller of the Mysteries, God's Seal Bearer, and the Lector Priest. They were responsible for the religious aspects of the proceedings. The first is often shown wearing the jackal-headed mask of Anubis, who was the god of mummification. These men consulted the sacred texts for the correct procedures, recited the ritual formulas, and supervised the work of a team of subordinate technicians, each of whom had his own task at each stage.

The line where the body was to be cut was marked by a priest called a scribe. Then the *paraschistes*, or ripper-

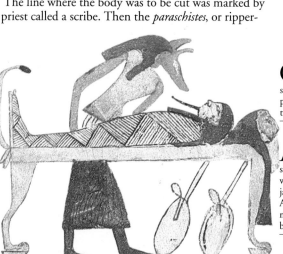

One of the few Anubis masks that have survived (above) is in painted terra-cotta, with two eye holes.

A detail from a sarcophagus (left) shows the embalmer, wearing the mask of the jackal-headed god Anubis, bending over the mummy, which lies on a bed shaped like a lion.

This Greco-Egyptian papyrus (left) shows a mummy on its way to the burial ground. The mummy is enclosed in a type of chest, which is carried on a barque, itself carried on a wheeled chariot hauled by a team of men—an innovation introduced at the end of the pharaonic era. The group is led by a priest carrying a censer.

up, made the incision for the removal of the viscera. He used a knife made either of flint or of obsidian, a naturally occurring volcanic glass that had to be imported into Egypt. The job of the *taricheutes*, the embalmer, was to desiccate the body using natron, while other specialists were responsible for its transportation and burial. The funeral service and, later on, the ceremony during which offerings were made, were conducted by designated priests.

All of the various artisans belonged to a guild and held an office that they could either sell or pass on to descendants or to a third party. Each of them had exclusive rights over a section of the population of a village or town, with the result that the necropolises were divided into sectors, and conflicts over the rights to a body frequently ensued.

The men who worked at the Pure Place were paid in kind—and, after about 700 BC, also in money—by the family of the deceased. Despite the importance of their role, they probably did not enjoy a high status in the community. They appear to have been obliged to live outside the town, no doubt on account of the peculiar nature of their activities.

The model of a funeral barque below was found in a Middle Kingdom tomb. Such barques serve as a reminder that the dead did indeed have to make a river crossing in order to reach their final resting place, since the burial grounds were located in the desert, on the western bank of the Nile.

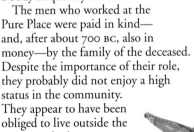

'**Y**ou will be like Ra, rising and setting through all eternity." The ancient Egyptians regarded death as a transition from one life to another. Mummification was the necessary preparation for entry into the eternal abode for man, woman, child, and animal alike.

CHAPTER III
TOWARD IMMORTALITY

Ancient Egyptians believed that the elements that combine in a human being come apart in death. In the illustrations here each mummy—dried and blackened—is accompanied by the *ba* of the living person —the bird-soul— which, through funerary magic, will ultimately reunite with the body.

To the ancient Egyptians every living creature was made up of a material structure, the body, to which were attached immaterial elements, including the *ba*, the equivalent of the soul or the personality, and the *ka*, the life force. In death these different elements became separated.

"Your Legs Will Carry You to the Eternal Abode and Your Hands Will Carry for You as Far as the Place of Infinite Duration"

In order to enter its second life, the body had to be reunited with the spiritual elements that had previously animated it. In other words it had to be preserved, and at every step of the mummification process, magic formulas reassured the dead person that his or her body was still intact. The destruction of the body was a very serious matter, signifying the impossibility of resurrection. Such a fear was perhaps behind the practice that began in the Old Kingdom of placing replicas of the dead person —either statues or "reserve heads," as they were known—in the tombs of kings and nobles; the heads served as magical replacements for a destroyed or damaged body.

Given the importance accorded to burial practices and monuments, one might be forgiven for assuming that the ancient Egyptians set little store by life itself. But in fact they regarded it as the most precious of all gifts. As one New Kingdom inscription reads, "Your happiness weighs more heavily than the life to come."

Death was viewed both as a simple transition from one life to the next and as a termination; it

An amulet in the shape of two frogs (left). The frog, a creature of the swamp (the primordial waters from which all life arose), was a symbol of eternal life.

Opposite: In the middle panel of this papyrus from the tomb of Tuthmosis III, the king is depicted as the sun god traveling across the sky in the solar barque. Baboons, the animals associated with Thoth, god of learning, are shown adoring the sun, with funerary divinities at prayer (upper panel). The rising sun is depicted as a scarab in its barque (lower panel).

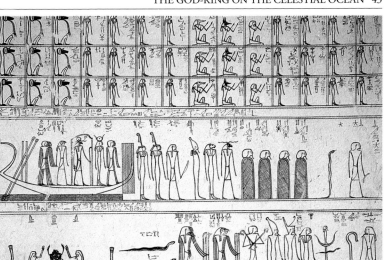

was the point of entry to "the place from which one never returns." In the Old Kingdom life after death was still, for most people, pictured in rather nebulous terms, with the king alone enjoying a privileged destiny. According to the stellar myth, he went to join the "fixed" (circumpolar) stars and live with the gods, with whom he became identified. In the solar myth he accompanied the sun on its course across the "celestial ocean" and participated in its daily rebirth. As far as ordinary men and women were concerned (though we have very little information), life after death probably consisted of a straightforward continuation of life on earth.

During the troubled 1st

Funerary statues like the ones opposite and left and reserve heads like the one above served as magical replacements for the body if the mummy was damaged. The name of the deceased was inscribed on the statue, since a name was thought to be imbued with life once it was written down.

Intermediate period (2181–2040 BC), a time of anarchy, provincial governors declared themselves equal in status to the king, and the ruling class, which was becoming increasingly powerful, laid claim to royal prerogatives in terms of immortality. Mummification and the religious formulas designed to ensure such immortality, originally the preserve of royalty, became available to increasing numbers of people. Many sought to be buried near Osiris's principal tomb, at Abydos, where the kings of the first dynasties had built themselves cenotaphs. Or, failing this, they had a stele erected there so that they could still continue to enjoy the protection of the god of the dead.

In the New Kingdom ordinary people adopted royal myths. On the coffin of a woman named Taneteret (above), the solar barque is preceded by Anubis.

A dead husband and wife in the afterlife, which is depicted as a continuation of earthly delights, with a table of offerings and a game of senet set in front of them.

"I Am Complete. I Am Justified. I Am Youthful. For, in Truth, I Am Osiris, Lord of all Eternity"

Ideas about what the afterlife entailed crystallized during the New Kingdom. The world of the dead was viewed as a subterranean kingdom ruled over by Osiris, as both king—his own experience of death and resurrection qualified him for the title of god of the dead—and the embodiment of the life

force. The most widespread myth told how Osiris reigned over Egypt before the first dynastic kings. He was murdered and dismembered by his brother Seth and then brought back to life by Isis, his sister and wife. Isis and Osiris had a son, Horus, and Horus was said to have vanquished Seth and then ascended the throne of Egypt, while Osiris descended to rule over the underworld. The fate of Osiris, who died and was then resurrected, became the model for every human death. Through the process of mummification, the preserved body became identified with the body of the god, and the dead person became an Osiris.

Immediately before it was placed in the tomb,

A statuette of Osiris made of gilded stone (left), showing him in all his majesty. He is equipped with his traditional attributes—wearing a shroud and the crown of Atef and holding the royal flail and crook. He has his arms crossed over his chest in a gesture frequently imitated by the embalmers.

A wall painting in the temple of Dendera showing Osiris on his funeral bed about to impregnate Isis, who hovers over him in the form of a bird. The product of this union was Horus, the royal protector (a living king was an incarnation of Horus; a dead king, an incarnation of Osiris). The bird on the right represents Nephthys, the sister of Isis.

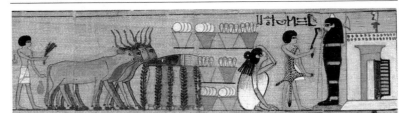

the mummified body, already resting in its coffin, was stood up in front of the door to the tomb, where it was given the "breath of life" by means of a ritual known as the Opening of the Mouth ceremony. Symbolically brought back to life, the mummy was then presented various offerings of food and deposited in the tomb, which would be its "dwelling place for millions of years."

The second life, which began at burial, is represented in great detail by New Kingdom illustrators and their successors. Anubis, keeper of the kingdom of the dead, led the dead person to receive judgment in the presence of Osiris, revealed now in all his glory. During judgment the dead person was obliged to recite the double "negative confession," declaring himself innocent of a whole series of crimes, both general and specific, against the gods and against humanity, proclaiming, among other things:

"I have not added to the weight of the scales.

"I have not carried away the milk from the mouths of children.

"I have not driven away the cattle which were upon their pastures."

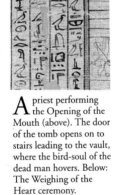

A priest performing the Opening of the Mouth (above). The door of the tomb opens on to stairs leading to the vault, where the bird-soul of the dead man hovers. Below: The Weighing of the Heart ceremony.

Next came the Weighing of the Heart. The heart, on one side of the balance, was supposed to be as light as a feather (symbol of the goddess Maat, the embodiment of truth and justice), but if it proved too heavy—if, in other words, the dead person's crimes outweighed his or her good deeds—the goddess Ammit the Gobbler was waiting open-mouthed to consume and consign the dead person to a second, and lasting, death. Thoth recorded the result of the weighing process in the presence of Osiris and other attendant gods.

The Dead Person Was Now "Justified" and Free to Undertake the Journey Through the Underworld

As a guide on the journey through the underworld the dead person had a copy of the *Book of the Dead* on a roll of papyrus, which was placed inside the coffin, on the mummy itself, or in a box serving as the pedestal of a statue of Osiris. This papyrus was illustrated with scenes constituting a sort of map of the afterlife. This was a world peopled with strange and terrifying creatures. The book also contained magic formulas instructing the dead person on how to overcome the obstacles that might lie ahead and how to find the way to the kingdom of the blessed.

The mere presence of

An illustration from the Hunefer *Book of the Dead* (above), showing the dead person (left) being led to judgment by Anubis and (right) standing before Osiris. In the center is the Weighing of the Heart ceremony. Below: Opet, the hippopotamus goddess, and Hathor, the cow goddess, emerging from the mountain of the West; illustration from the Ani *Book of the Dead*.

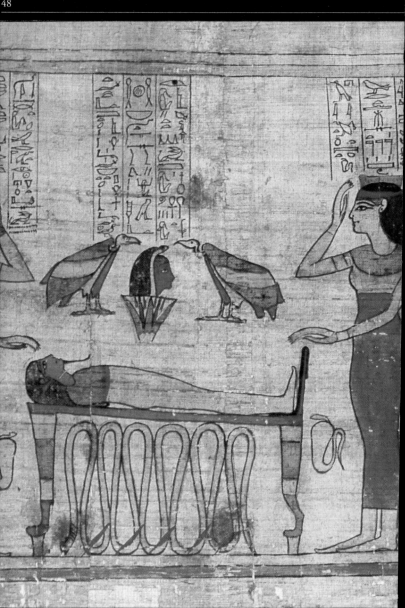

Journey to the Kingdom of the Dead

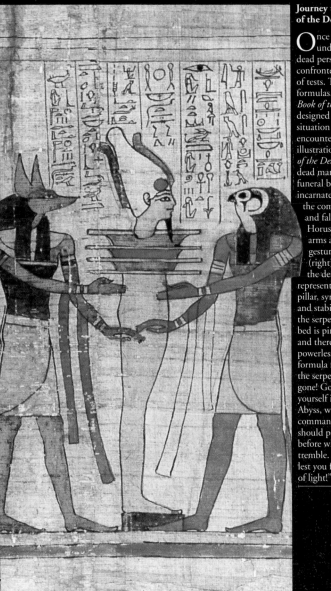

Once in the underworld the dead person was confronted with a series of tests. The magic formulas contained in the *Book of the Dead* were designed to help in any situation that might be encountered. This illustration from the *Book of the Dead* shows the dead man lying on his funeral bed (left) and incarnated as Osiris in the company of Anubis and falcon-headed Horus, who place their arms around him in a gesture of protection (right). The body of the dead man is represented as the *djed* pillar, symbol of strength and stability. Note how the serpent beneath the bed is pinned with knives and thereby rendered powerless. The book's formula for banishing the serpent runs: "Be gone! Go and drown yourself in the lake of the Abyss, where your father commanded that you should perish! I am Ra, before whom men tremble. Be gone, rebel, lest you feel his knives of light!"

this book alongside the mummy was sufficient to ensure its survival in the afterlife. Other funerary books of a more theological nature—the *Book of Gates*, the *Book of Caverns*, and the *Book of Douat* [the kingdom of the dead] *and What It Contains*—were reserved for royal tombs and served merely as decoration.

The *Book of the Dead*, which first appeared in the New Kingdom, brought together a number of ancient traditions, from the Coffin Texts, inscribed on the walls

"I have acquired this field.... Here I eat and drink and feast; here I plough and I harvest," says the *Book of the Dead*. Below: An illustration from the Ani *Book of the Dead* depicting life in the other world.

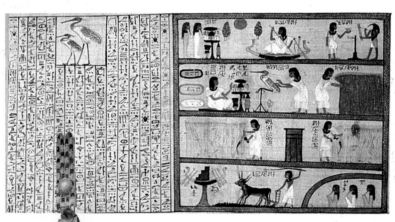

of Middle Kingdom sarcophagi, to the Pyramid Texts, engraved on the walls of the mortuary chambers in the royal pyramids from the 5th dynasty (c. 2494–2345 BC) on. Originally reserved for the king, the Pyramid Texts were gradually adapted for universal use. There are many versions of the *Book of the Dead;* no single papyrus contains every verse.

A richly decorated sarcophagus for a falcon (left) is topped by a statue of the bird wearing the plumed crown of Horus. Other sarcophagi might be carved in the shape of the animal they housed.

Opposite: Two falcon mummies. The one on the right is wearing a mask and is as intricately wrapped as any human mummy; the one on the left is altogether more simple.

Animals, Too

Many tombs housed animal as well as human occupants.

A baboon was discovered, for example, in the tomb of a Theban priestess of the 21st dynasty, and more modest tombs housed dogs, cats, and birds—probably household pets that their owners wished to keep with them in the afterlife. Some animals even had their own coffin: The favorite cat of Prince Tuthmosis, eldest son of Amenophis III, was buried in a limestone sarcophagus (discovered at Memphis) bearing the inscription "Osiris Ta-miat the Justified One."

The ancient Egyptians saw nothing odd about mummifying animals: They made no essential distinction between humans and animals, and their lives were closely interwoven.

Gods Could Take Animal or Human Form

Animal worship was a permanent feature of Egyptian civilization. Gods might assume different forms at different periods in history, but their essential attributes remained the same. Thus, the falcon Horus, an ancient incarnation of royal power, was sometimes represented as the bird itself and sometimes as a man with a bird's head. The Apis Bull, at Memphis, and the Ram of Mendes and the Ram of Elephantine, on the other hand, retained their animal form throughout the course of ancient Egyptian civilization.

These animals, regarded as living gods, were therefore destined for immortality through mummification. They were unique. There was only one Apis Bull, recognizable by distinctive markings on his hide. He had his own temple where he was worshiped and a sacred living enclosure where his followers came to see him. When he died he was mummified, and the funeral rites resembled those performed at human burials. His

remains were deposited in a massive granite sarcophagus, placed originally in an individual tomb and then, later on, in a huge collective vault—the famous Serapeum at Saqqara. The necropolis dedicated to the Sacred Cows, the Mothers of Apis, was located nearby. Worship and funerary rites were similar in the case of the Mnevis Bull at Heliopolis, the Buchis Bull at Armant, the Ram of Mendes, and the Ram of Elephantine, also regarded as living gods. The crocodile god Sobek was worshiped in the Fayuum and at Kom Ombo, and Sobek temples housed sacred crocodiles, one of which may have been regarded as the incarnation of the god himself. Herodotus describes how the people of Thebes and the Fayuum each had their own tame crocodile, which they fed and looked after. The crocodile wore earrings and bracelets on its front legs and was given sacred food. Strabo, writing four centuries later, adds: "The sacred

Ibises were mummified by the thousands. Left: A watercolor of a mummified ibis in the *Description of Egypt*, with, beside it, a photograph of a ceramic pot containing several ibises.

A detail from a stele in the Buchis necropolis showing the Buchis Bull, incarnation of the god Monthu, receiving offerings from Ptolemy V Epiphanes. An inscription states that the bull died at the age of thirteen years, ten months, and twenty-eight days.

crocodile is fed in a lake of its own; the priests know how to tame it and they call it Soukos [Sobek]."

Certain Animals Were Associated with Particular Gods— For Example, the Cat with Bastet and the Ibis and the Baboon with Thoth

The hundreds of thousands of ibis and cat mummies discovered in the necropolises were apparently offerings bought specially by pilgrims to be mummified and presented to their respective gods. The temple to the goddess Bastet at Bubastis and that of the god Thoth at Hermopolis reared sacred cats and ibises, it seems, expressly for sacrificial purposes—a practice that became very widespread during the first millennium BC. Other animals were treated in the same way.

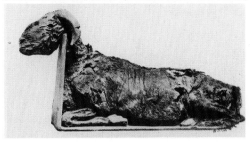

A rather different case is presented by the mummy of a frog found in a tomb in the village of Duch, resting between the thighs of a castrated and mummified adult male. According to one version of the myth, when Osiris was dismembered, his penis was thrown into the Nile and was then devoured by fish. The Duch mummy appears to have been modeled on this myth. The presence of the frog, which is a symbol of rebirth, affirms the belief in the future life of the dead man.

Three stages in the unwrapping of the mummy of a ram from the town of Elephantine, whose principal deity was the ram-god Khnum.

To facilitate life in the other world, the ancient Egyptians furnished their dead with offerings, some of which were of considerable value. The direct consequence of this—the pillaging of tombs—was to become a national pastime, and was a fate that few tombs, however simple, escaped.

CHAPTER IV
FROM ETERNAL LIFE TO HARSH REALITY

Eyes painted on a Middle Kingdom coffin (left) allowed the dead to see. Opposite: The King's Chamber in the Great Pyramid, painted by Luigi Mayer in the early 19th century. The granite sarcophagus there, of the pharaoh Cheops, was found empty.

So impressive are the funerary monuments and their contents that one is forced to conclude that the ancient Egyptians devoted a major part of their resources to setting up their eternal homes. The royal tombs provide the most obvious illustration of this. Incredible energy and considerable financial resources went into the construction of the pyramids and the burial vaults in the Valley of the Kings, not to mention the funerary temples, such as Chephren's Valley Temple, and the Ramesseum and Medinet Habu of Ramses II and III respectively. The sums spent on constructing tombs for the average man and woman were also proportionally large.

Sennedjem's tomb at Deir el-Medina (below) is in typical New Kingdom style, with underground vaults and complex superstructures. Note the funerary chapel surmounted by a small pyramid (left), the temple-facade gateway (right), and the deep shaft equipped with handholds leading to the underground chambers.

Tomb Architecture Varied Little Over the Centuries, with Few Basic Types

Tomb styles depended on local topography and the financial resources of the owner. Simple burials in graves are found in every period, but the more complex tombs underwent some evolution. Mastabas—low rectangular buildings over tomb shafts—were built during the Old and the Middle Kingdoms, and rock-cut tombs made their first appearance at the end of the Old Kingdom. Tombs with a pyramidal superstructure—the most sophisticated of which are the royal pyramids of the Old

Two different types of royal tomb: Chephren's pyramid (4th dynasty, opposite); Queen Merneith's mastaba (1st dynasty, left) at Saqqara.

Kingdom (such as those of the pharaohs Cheops, Chephren, and Mykerinus)—were still being built as private tombs during the New Kingdom, albeit on a much more modest scale. The same style was adopted at Meroë in Upper Nubia. One final innovation was the tomb with a chapel added, first built in the New Kingdom.

The Tomb Was the Dead Person's New Habitat, a World Governed by Magic, Where Existence Continues, but in a Different Way

The environment of everyday life simply had to be represented in various ways for the dead person to continue to enjoy it. Traditional images show the deceased sitting in front of a table laden with food, and hunting and farming scenes may have a similar significance, though they may merely have been intended to

Early-19th-century adventurers had no qualms about removing coffins and valuable objects from the depths of burial chambers like the one at Gourna (pictured in cross section below). Sculptor Jean-Jacques Rifaud, who spent forty years in Egypt, indicates on the drawing how he managed to maneuver the coffin up to the surface.

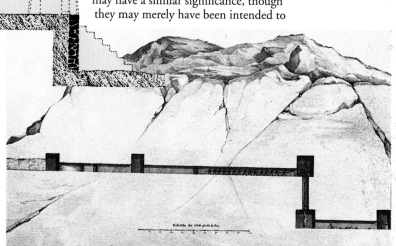

evoke real life in general, rather than particular personal circumstances.

For the same reason the dead are always represented as young and in full possession of their faculties. This was particularly true in the case of the pharaohs —who began work on their tombs more or less as soon as they came to power, while they were in fact still relatively young. Models evoking various activities of daily life and miniature

Royal tombs, like that of Seti I at Thebes (above), were decorated with scenes of primarily religious inspiration. Images from everyday life tended to be reserved for the ordinary man and woman. This detail (left) from one woman's stele shows her seated in front of a table laden with bread.

houses—"soul houses"—are frequently encountered in the tombs of ordinary people from the Middle Kingdom and are a further reminder that the dead person continued to "live" in a real sense.

"Offerings Will Be Made and Provisions of Bread, Beer, Meat, Poultry, and Incense Will Be Given"

Offerings of food ensured the dead person's survival in the afterlife. But the dead were also surrounded with other useful objects from daily life—items of toiletry, clothes, and fabric, pottery and stone vessels, arms—as in the case of Tutankhamun's weapons and Amenophis II's bow. Tools relating to specific trades, such as writing materials, medical papyri, shuttles and spindles, and even toys were also included.

While many of these objects would have been used by the dead person in real life, others had a merely ceremonial function. Tutankhamun's golden chariot, for example, had clearly never been used.

The Tomb Also Housed a Range of Ritual Objects

Tomb contents included Canopic jars and ushabtis, which were most widely used from the Middle Kingdom on. In the New Kingdom it became customary to place several hundred of these figurines near the coffin (one for each day of the year, with "overseers" to supervise them). As servants of the dead person, the ushabtis were

Food was mummified before being offered to the dead, as in the case of this basket of legs of lamb (above left) found in a tomb at Deir el-Bahari. Objects from daily life and models representing the life of the dead person were also placed in the tomb. Above: A bronze mirror; below: a model of a granary with cows.

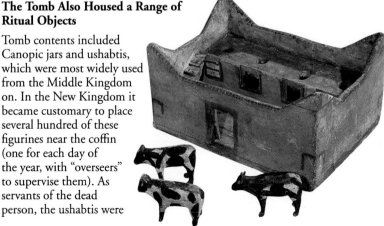

supposed to undertake any tasks Osiris imposed on their owner in the life hereafter.

From the Middle Kingdom until the Greco-Roman period, nude female figures with exaggerated sexual characteristics were placed in tombs belonging to both men and women. Described as "concubines of the dead," they were probably intended to facilitate sexual functioning in the afterlife.

"If any one of you is required to carry out a task in the other world, you will say 'Present!'" These words from the *Book of the Dead* were often inscribed on the ushabtis, as if to remind them of their role as servants of the dead. These figurines vary in height from a few inches to a foot or more, depending on the importance of their owner, and some, like the one above belonging to Amenhotep, have their own miniature coffin in imitation of their owner's. Above left: A chest containing Canopic jars belonging to a person named Psametik, with the divine guardians of the viscera represented on the outside. Below: Ushabtis belonging to a person named Neferibre.

The Mummy Was Encased in a Series of Protective Containers, the Elaborateness of Which Depended on the Wealth of the Dead Person

The outermost container was either a stone sarcophagus —for kings or important officials—or, more often, a wooden coffin. These were of either rectangular or anthropoid design. The decoration of the sarcophagus or coffin varied considerably over the centuries and included ritual texts, mythological scenes, and biographical details, including the dead person's name, status, and occupation.

The sarcophagus originally contained a second, anthropoid coffin, which was usually made of wood. Beginning in the 22nd dynasty (c. 945 BC), this second coffin was replaced by a cartonnage, which was made of

The first coffins were plain boxes made of wood or, in the case of pharaohs and important officials, stone, and sometimes had very thick sides (a stone sarcophagus could weigh several tons). Decoration, in the form of symbolic motifs and funerary texts, was introduced during the second half of the 2nd millennium BC, and the name of the dead person was inscribed henceforth on the coffin lid. Anthropoid coffins— imitating, however

layers of linen or papyrus stiffened with glue or plaster and decorated with brightly colored motifs frequently set off with gold. In the majority of cartonnages, the lines of the body are barely suggested, while the facial features, framed by a heavy wig, are often highly expressive, if also often stereotyped. The pharaohs, and a few very wealthy individuals, had a third coffin, and the pharaohs also had a solid gold mask (those belonging to Psousennes and Tutankhamun have survived to this day). Finally came the mummy itself, wrapped in its layers of shrouds and

crudely, the shape of their occupant—were also introduced. Menuf's sarcophagus (above), is of this type. Practically every sarcophagus and coffin had been opened before archaeologists arrived on the scene.

These three richly decorated coffins belonged to a certain Tamutnefret, plainly a woman of some standing. The coffin lids are decorated with bands of text and depictions of funerary deities, including a winged goddess who envelops the dead woman in a gesture of protection. The inclusion of the funerary texts was a means of ensuring the dead person's continued existence in the afterlife.

bandages.

Only wealthier individuals could afford both coffins and cartonnages. Many people were buried without either, but were simply wrapped in their shrouds and bandages (and the poorest folk were not mummified at all). In the late period it was common for mummies to wear only a gilded and painted plaster mask, and from the Greco-Roman period on a portrait painted in wax on wood was inserted inside the bandages wrapping the face. These are the so-called Fayuum portraits, named for the place they were first found.

The mummy was now fully prepared and equipped for the afterlife and ready to enter the tomb—its "dwelling

The painted shrouds of the Greco-Roman period were relatively stiff and were designed to cover the entire mummy once it had been bandaged. Left: A shroud painted with a traditional scene from the *Book of the Dead,* showing the dead person, in classical costume, being presented to Osiris by Anubis.

During the Ptolemaic period (305–30 BC), cartonnages evolved into plaques decorated with funerary motifs and protective symbols, attached directly to the shroud. This type of cartonnage always included a large floral collar (flowers were a symbol of renewal) and a "foot box," as seen here.

place for millions of years." The dead still had to be protected from one thing, however, and that was the aggression and greed of those people still in the world of the living.

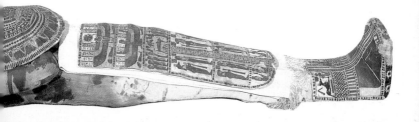

The Dead Who Look at Us

There was a new emphasis on realism in the presentation of mummies in Greco-Roman Egypt, as if it had become important for the dead person to be recognized easily. Mummy portraits, such as these of a man named Ammonius and an unknown woman (opposite and left), were painted on wood or cloth with colored wax or pigments mixed with a binding agent. The range of facial types, some very expressive, is a reflection of a highly cosmopolitan population. These paintings, which have no precedent in ancient Egypt, recall the Roman portraits found at Pompeii. Masks like the one above also date from this period and are quite different in style from traditional Egyptian masks.

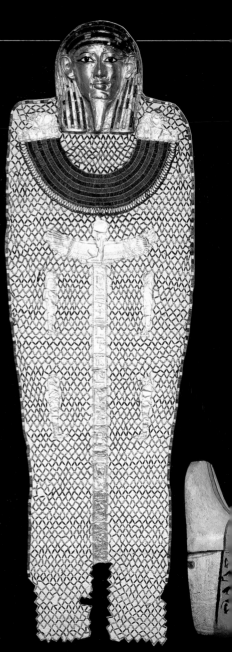

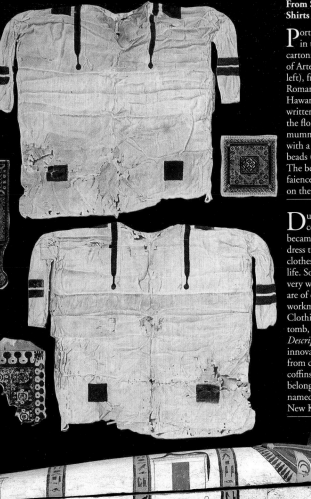

From Sarcophagi to Shirts

Portraits were inserted in the bandages or the cartonnage, as in the case of Artemidorus (opposite left), from the Greco-Roman cemetery at Hawara (his name is written in Greek below the floral garland). Some mummies were covered with a net of colored beads (opposite right). The beads were made of faience or simply painted on the cartonnage.

During the 4th century AD, it became customary to dress the dead in the clothes they had worn in life. Some of these are very well preserved and are of excellent workmanship. Left: Clothing found in a tomb, from the *Description of Egypt*. Such innovations were a far cry from classical Egyptian coffins like the one below, belonging to a woman named Madja of the New Kingdom.

What Happened to the Mummies?

The looting of tombs became a widespread practice early on, and the Egyptians adopted increasingly sophisticated measures in an attempt to deter potential robbers. A vigorous race between tomb architects and robbers, the architects trying to stay one step ahead, continued from the first dynasties right up until the end of ancient Egyptian civilization.

While the pyramids were lavishly equipped with magnificent funerary goods, to mount a direct assault on one was clearly no easy matter and in practice could be done only with the help of the guards. With the weakening of the central powers and the unrest that characterized the 1st Intermediate period, however, the pyramids were no longer safe from intruders. Breaking into one could still not have been an easy task, given the internal security arrangements—portcullises, false corridors, and concealed openings, many of them sealed with blocks of stone—and yet every pyramid was broken into, and by the time the archaeologists arrived the funerary chambers were virtually stripped bare.

In the New Kingdom, for religious but also for security reasons, the pharaohs abandoned the pyramid —which was such an obvious focal point—in favor of

Opposite: The catacombs at Alexandria, showing the square-sided pillars and Greek pediment typical of tombs in this region.

Tutankhamun's is the only royal tomb to have remained substantially intact until modern times. It was broken into shortly after the king was buried, but luckily the intruders were disturbed. The photographs below and opposite show how the tomb looked when it was opened in 1922. Funerary goods were piled and scattered in disarray, and one of the intruders had left his footprints on a chest (below).

Mummies excavated at the beginning of the 20th century (left).

Above: A detail from the Abbott Papyrus, a record of a lawsuit brought against the looters of Ramses II's tomb in the reign of Ramses IX. Several arrests were made, and the defendants admitted they had gone "to steal from the tombs as [they were] accustomed to do." They had opened the coffins of a king and a queen, removed the amulets, jewels, and other precious objects, and then set fire to the coffins.

more discreet underground burial chambers. Vast tombs were tunneled in secret (at least initially) in the limestone cliffs overlooking the Valley of the Kings and the Valley of the Queens, and the entrance to each tomb was generally concealed. But, despite the presence of a permanent guard and despite the internal arrangements—deep shafts, dead ends, enormously heavy granite sarcophagi, which were virtually impenetrable —these tombs were looted just like their predecessors.

The proof of this looting is contained in the fragmentary records of an action brought against looters in the reign of Ramses IX (1131–1112 BC). Although nothing can be confirmed, there are hints in the robbers' statements that point to collusion at a high level, possibly even implicating the chief of police in charge of the necropolis.

In the course of the following years increasing numbers of tombs were violated, notably those of Seti I and Ramses II in the Valley of the Kings. Eventually, between 1070 and 945 BC, the high priests of Amun had the royal mummies of the 18th, 19th, and 20th dynasties exhumed and reburied in secret caches, whose whereabouts were not discovered until the end of the 19th century. Inevitably most of these mummies had been stripped of valuables and had to be bandaged again for reburial.

In a Greco-Roman tomb at Duch, a letter dating from the last century concerning a supply of hay for a donkey was found—evidently left behind by a careless thief. In another case the intruder had been crushed when part of the roof of the tomb had caved in, and his skeleton ended up keeping company with the mummies he had come to rob.

Emptying the tomb of Tutankhamun (below) was a painstaking operation, and some of the objects were restored on site. The entire collection is housed today in the Cairo Museum.

Tomb 20 in the necropolis at Duch (left), with its piles of bodies, furniture, and funeral cloth, presents a scene similar to that in a watercolor by Sir John Gardner Wilkinson (opposite) of a peasant woman searching for antiquities in a tomb at Thebes (c. 1830).

Private Tombs Were Also Looted

If it is not altogether surprising that royal tombs, widely known to conceal fabulous riches, were looted, one might have hoped that tombs belonging to ordinary men and women would be spared. On the whole, however, since early antiquity, even the poorest private tombs were broken into. The official inquiry conducted under Ramses IX shows that all the civil tombs inspected had been violated.

It may seem curious that the ancient Egyptians, who are known to have been deeply religious, apparently had no qualms about depriving the dead of their means of survival in the other world. But it probably came down to simple need: No doubt, for people struggling to survive, the temptation of the riches was simply too great, particularly during times of economic hardship, and, rather than professional thieves, the looters were often artisans and peasants working in the vicinity of the necropolises. The practice of pillaging

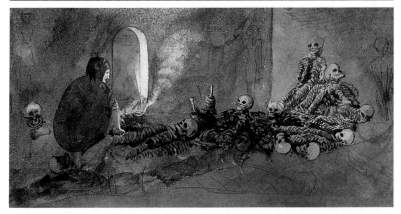

tombs continued up until modern times, supplying the illegal trade in antiquities and destroying irreplaceable archaeological material.

And Ancient Tombs Were Reused

Reusing tombs was a fairly common practice, at least in the late period, and it is not unusual to find tombs built for a single family piled high with mummies. Even the tombs of queens were subjected to this indignity, which usually led to the deterioration of the original occupants.

The pharaohs themselves set the precedent by "recycling" sarcophagi, funerary goods, and even tombs. A lion with a man's head from Tanis bears no fewer than three different royal inscriptions and Psousennes I (21st dynasty) was buried in a sarcophagus that had originally housed an official of the 19th.

Mummies were unwrapped, stripped of their coverings and jewels, and often removed from their supposed "dwelling place for millions of years." Needless to say many of them failed to survive the ordeal.

In the 19th century Cairo was full of people selling figurines, amulets, and jewelry to tourists (below and opposite). More valuable items were sold by established antiquarians, who had a network of contacts.

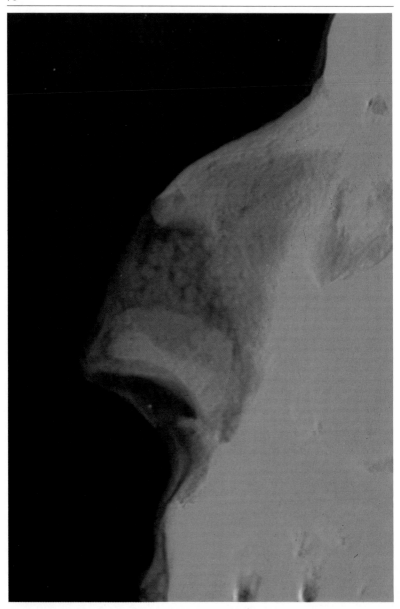

The birth of Egyptology produced a gradual revival of interest in mummies. Originally no more than objects of curiosity or raw material for pharmaceutical purposes, they became an important focus of scientific study. Archaeologists have saved many from the hands of looters, and today, with the help of modern technology, they are engaged in trying to analyze and preserve this irreplaceable human material.

CHAPTER V
UNDER EXPERT ANALYSIS

An X-ray of Ramses II's nose (opposite). The mass of dark specks is comprised of grains of pepper, used as a preservative by the embalmers. The bonelike object above the nostril is in fact a plug of solidified resin designed to hold the pepper in place. Right: A mummy's arm, a watercolor from the *Description of Egypt*.

Throughout the 19th century the
unwrapping of mummies was an
occasion for special ceremonies to
which a select public was invited, but
these gatherings were more like
entertainment (of a rather morbid
kind) than serious scientific inquiry.
Things changed with the sensational
discovery of the cache of royal
mummies at Deir el-Bahari in July
1881. These illustrious mummies
had to be conserved at all costs, and
a new investigative approach was
called for (though, as it happened,
the unbandaging was carried out in
a rather hasty and unceremonious
fashion). The mummies were first
housed in the museum in the
Cairo suburb of Bulaq, and then,
in 1902, they were transferred to
the newly built Cairo Museum.

From this time on the
unbandaging was often
followed by a more or less
complete autopsy. From this,
information could be pieced

together about the mummification process. Also any ailments or accidents suffered by the living person could be diagnosed from the mummified remains.

In 1895 the German physicist Wilhelm Conrad Röntgen discovered the X-ray, and, on 8 November of the same year, he took an X-ray (the exposure time was half an hour) of his wife's hand. (This discovery won Röntgen the first Nobel prize for physics, in 1901.) The great English archaeologist Sir William Matthew Flinders Petrie soon recognized the importance of the X-ray technique for Egyptology and took the first X-rays of mummies in 1896.

At Last Egyptologists Gained Access to a Means of Exploring Mummified Human Remains Without Harming Them: Radiology

Radiographic equipment was not yet powerful enough, however, to do more than X-ray the body's extremities, and when, in 1912, Sir Grafton Elliot Smith published the first exhaustive description of the royal mummies conserved in Cairo, X-ray information formed only a small part of his findings. There was a major logistical difficulty in using

Sarcophagi and Canopic jars (center) at the museum at Bulaq, founded by Auguste Mariette (1821–81) in 1858. Mariette also discovered the Serapeum at Saqqara and founded the Egyptian Antiquities Service in an attempt to halt the pillaging of ancient monuments.

Opposite above: Arthur Mace (1874–1928, left) cleaning an artifact in the tomb of Seti II at Luxor, and Sir Gaston Maspero (right), Mariette's successor at Bulaq. Maspero's excavations included the pyramids of Giza and the temple at Luxor.

Above: Sir William Matthew Flinders Petrie (seated, center) with his wife and assistants. He was the outstanding figure in Egyptian archaeology at the turn of the century.

X-rays: How to bring together, physically, the radiologist, the equipment, and the mummy itself. Tuthmosis IV's mummy, for example, had to be taken by taxi to the hospital housing the first radiology unit in Cairo.

As X-ray techniques improved, interest in radiology grew. In 1913 scientists described the first lumbar-sacral abnormality observed in a mummy (this type of abnormality, widely encountered today, is responsible for sciatic pain and lumbago). In 1931 Roy L. Moodie was able to record radiographic information for seventeen mummies, and by 1967 P. H. K. Gray had studied a total of 133 mummies conserved in various European museums, notably in Great Britain and the Netherlands.

Above: Photographs of Tuthmosis II (right) and, possibly, Tuthmosis I (left). Despite an apparent family likeness, X-rays indicate that the latter skeleton probably belongs in fact to a man much younger than the pharaoh is thought to have been.

James Harris and Kent Weeks Began a Careful Study of the Royal Mummies in the Cairo Museum

By identifying illnesses or physical characteristics, the research of these scholars, published in 1973 and 1980, has authenticated such details as family links and confirmed some details of the ancient texts. For example, Seqenenre II, a pharaoh of the 16th century BC, is said to have met his death on the battlefield—a fact that is corroborated both by the terrible head wounds discovered on his mummy and X-ray confirmation of violent impact to the cranium.

X-ray studies have also cast doubt on some previously accepted identifications. The skeleton of the mummy thought to be that of Tuthmosis I (1504–1492 BC) has remnants of cartilage at the end of the long bones, a sign that the body was still growing at the time of death. The dead person could have been no more than eighteen—an age incompatible with the length of reign of this pharaoh. Another strange detail is the way the mummy's hands are placed in front of the genitalia; none of Tuthmosis' successors have their hands in this position.

Opposite: In 1926 two French journalists X-rayed a mummy with a small portable X-ray machine at the Musée Guimet d'Histoire Naturelle, Lyons. The X-rays revealed an abnormal mass in the trunk; this was almost certainly a mixture of earth, resin, and spices inserted in place of the viscera.

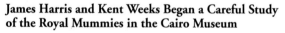

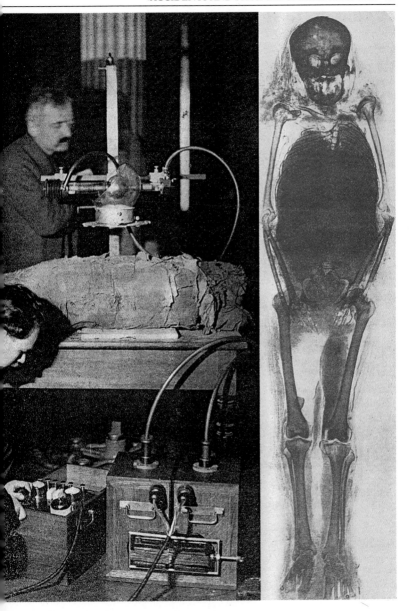

Today Numerous Other Techniques Are Used in the Study of Mummies

Besides radiology, histology (the science of organic tissues), the study of blood and tissue groups, endoscopy, and a whole range of chemical and physical microanalyses are now available for studying mummies. In addition, there are more recent techniques such as medical imaging, in particular,

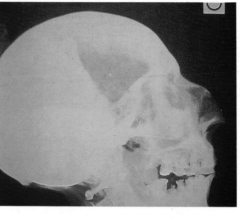

CT scanning. Magnetic resonance imaging (MRI), on the other hand, cannot be used on mummies, since it depends on hydrogen atoms, which in the human body are found in the form of water, and are therefore absent in mummies.

Although it can provide interesting information, radiocarbon dating is not yet sufficiently precise for the purposes of estimating the exact age of human tissue. Another method, involving the study of amino acids, can also make a contribution to this field. Its advantage over radiocarbon dating is that it can be applied to very small samples of material, but its reliability depends on the temperature at which the material for analysis was conserved.

Several teams worldwide have conducted particularly worthwhile

In 1976, 3200 years after his death, Ramses II was taken to Paris for treatment. It was the first time that a royal mummy had left Egyptian soil, and archaeologists made full use of the opportunity by subjecting it to an exhaustive examination. The X-ray of Ramses' skull (above) shows that his brain had been removed and the cranial cavity filled with resin. His teeth were in very poor condition, which was hardly surprising: at the time of his death, Ramses was probably around eighty years old.

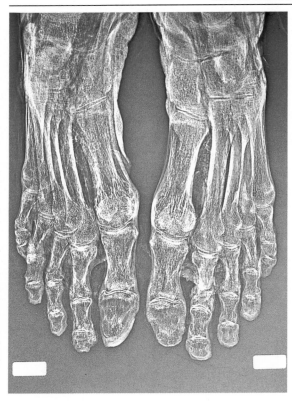

R amses II suffered from arteriosclerosis. This image (left) shows arterial calcification (visible as more or less continuous white lines) between the first and second metatarsal bones of the pharaoh's feet. Calcification was also found in other parts of the body, notably the carotid arteries. In addition, the photograph revealed a fracture to the cervical spine. Although statues and images in the temples show Ramses holding his head up very straight, even a little stiffly, the neck of his mummy (see below opposite) has a pronounced curvature, probably caused by the embalmers. They were not, however, responsible for the fact that Ramses' arms do not lie neatly across his chest. After thousands of years underground, when exposed to the air and the heat, the tissues of the arms became deformed, and they moved out of alignment. Once it had been restored and partly rebandaged, the mummy was sterilized by radiation and replaced in the wooden coffin in which it was first found (overleaf).

work in recent years. For instance, a team at the University of Pennsylvania led by Aidan Cockburn has carried out an exhaustive study of four anonymous mummies, christened PUM (Pennsylvania University Museum) I–IV. Findings for the first three mummies were rather disappointing, but PUM IV has provided a wealth of information, particularly regarding human tissue. In 1976 a French team under the direction of Lionel Balout and Colette Roubet took on the job of restoring and studying the mummy of Ramses II, and an English team at the University of Manchester, led by Rosalie David, has studied a series of seventeen mummies dating from the New Kingdom to the Greco-Roman period.

Anthropologists, meanwhile, have been conducting their own studies of the many skeletons discovered in the necropolises, and their findings have demonstrated the weakness inherent in studying mummies in museums. In such collections both the provenance and the date of the mummies tends to be uncertain, and because of their small number and their diversity they are not representative of a natural population, unlike the large homogeneous groups studied by the anthropologists. For this reason some archaeologists have now adopted the approach of X-raying mummies on site, where they can be said to form part of a statistically uniform population.

What Can Be Learned from Studying Mummies

As regards the actual technique of mummification, all the recent studies confirm what Herodotus—almost the only, and certainly the best, written source until modern times—had to say on the subject. Mummies examined by modern archaeologists vary in terms of workmanship and quality, in line with the three categories Herodotus described. They range from those

Roger Lichtenberg X-raying a mummy on site (at Duch)—a task that often calls for imagination and a talent for improvisation. Below: Cleaning sand from a mummy. This is a painstaking job that can take half a day.

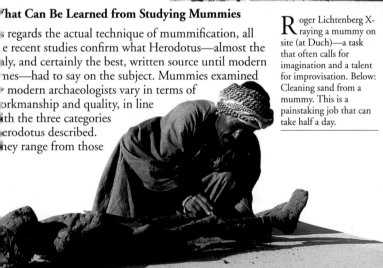

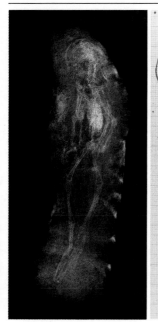

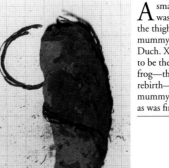

A small package (left) was found between the thighs of a castrated mummy in a tomb at Duch. X-rays showed it to be the mummy of a frog—the symbol of rebirth—and not the mummy's sexual organs, as was first supposed.

that benefited from "first-class" techniques —which have preserved the body intact and retained facial expressiveness—to those mummies—the product of more hurried or even slapdash techniques—that have deteriorated to a greater or lesser degree and are now incomplete or damaged.

Other observations tally with ritual prescriptions or what we know from myth. The Osirian arms-crossed position is one example; some other mummies are castrated, in allusion to the same myth. Traces of gold have been found on the face and limbs of some mummies. This type of body gilding was a late deification practice that was supposed to turn the dead person into an Osiris: A ritual formula runs, "You are regenerated by gold."

In some cases the embalmer appears to have been simply concentrating on achieving the most attractive results. For example, he might have patched together a

Gold leaf or electrum was applied to the face (above, the "priest of Duch") or other parts of the body in the Greco-Roman period. As a stable metal, gold would have helped to prevent deterioration.

damaged hand, and where a tooth was missing he might have inserted an ivory one on a wooden peg. Or again he might place a small onion in an eye socket to give the dead person the appearance of sight (this may in fact have been in accordance with ritual practices specified in the embalmers' handbooks).

The position of the disemboweling incision appears to have had no religious significance: It was originally made on the lower left-hand side of the body, at a right angle to the ribs, and then, following Tuthmosis III's reign (1479–1425 BC), it was cut parallel to the pubic bone. The opening was not generally sewn up. In some cases no incision was made at all, and the abdominal organs were removed via the rectum.

The scenes depicted on sarcophagi and tombs tell us a great deal about the precise techniques used by the embalmers, though one aspect that is virtually never illustrated is the desiccation process. Below: Detail from the Hildesheim sarcophagus showing a mummified body being sprinkled with water to remove any remaining natron crystals and impurities.

For many years archaeologists were in doubt as to whether the natron used to desiccate the body was applied as a solution or in the form of crystals. It became apparent, however, from studies carried out by Alfred Lucas, who experimented with the mummification of pigeons, and by Dr. Zaki Iskander, using ducks, that it must have been natron crystals that were used (no doubt in such a way as to completely cover the body).

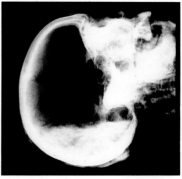

The ancient texts do not specify precisely what balms and unguents were used, and their chemical makeup is very difficult to establish because of the profound modifications that the molecules have undergone over the course of time. They are variously referred to as "resin," "bitumen" (the word *mummy* derives from an Arabic word for bitumen), and "cedarwood oil." The aromatic plants discovered both in and on the mummies have been easier to identify; they include laurel, pepper, cistus, and juniper.

CT scans are more precise than X-rays, particularly where soft tissue is concerned. Scanning is useful for studying the thorax and the abdomen, since in an X-ray the replaced viscera or the products used for stuffing the body show up only as a dark, undifferentiated mass. Above: A section of the skull of a mummy showing the block of resin inserted in place of the brain.

Mummies Provide a Unique Research Opportunity for Supplementing Anthropological Studies

Most anthropological studies relating to the ancient Egyptians have been carried out on skeletal remains, but mummies can provide a wealth of information not otherwise available. By studying hair, nails, skin, and fingerprints, we can learn a great deal about ethnic categories and

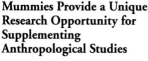

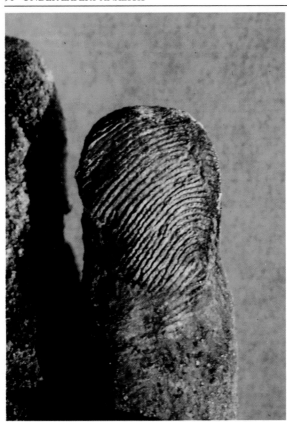

Through careful mummification even the most delicate anatomical structures were preserved. Left: A fingertip (magnification: 3.5x) showing the fingerprint and the openings of the sweat glands.

An X-ray (opposite above) of part of the femurs and the knee joints of a mummy, showing the lines relating to arrested growth due to malnourishment or illness.

Opposite below: The deformed left foot of the pharaoh Siptah (end of the 19th dynasty). Experts are divided. Some think it was a club foot, while others see it as a consequence of polio.

gain a fairly good idea of what the ancient Egyptians actually looked like.

Archaeologists have now established a method of scientifically measuring the bones of mummies on site using X-rays. They have also successfully carried out studies on mummified tissue. Their findings confirm the historical hypothesis that the ancient Egyptians were descended in roughly equal measures from Berber and Semitic peoples, with an increasing Negroid influence from the north to the south of the country. It is particularly striking that, despite various external influences at different periods of their history, the Egyptian people have remained remarkably unchanged to modern times.

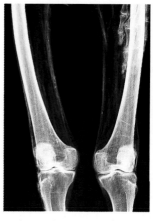

Mummies Are a Much More Fruitful Source of Information than Skeletons for Studying the State of Health of a Population

The study of X-ray photographs has also yielded useful statistics concerning the striae, or linear marks, found on bones, which are evidence of arrested growth. These marks, corresponding to periods of illness or malnourishment, are frequently found on mummies analyzed at the necropolis at Duch, which was in a particularly poor area.

Other studies have established that the average lifespan of people in Egypt in the first centuries AD was approximately forty years—which is only a few years less than in Europe 150 years ago. However, this figure fails to take into account the high rate of death at birth and the high infant mortality rate.

Dental studies show widespread abrasion of the crowns —which is hardly surprising when it is known that the ancient Egyptians ate a type of bread made with coarse flour containing sand. This wearing down of the teeth led to gum damage and extensive abscesses. Tooth decay, on the other hand, became a problem only fairly late in Egyptian history, when sugar began to show up in the diet, first only in the ruling classes. Honey had long been known and used in Egypt and was even one of the ingredients of a recommended remedy for tooth decay.

The ancient medical papyri list a number of illnesses to which the Egyptians were prone, but many of them are difficult to identify from the texts alone. The study of mummies helps to clarify the nature of some of these illnesses and confirms the identification of others, while also pointing to the presence of some that were not mentioned in the texts. Injuries, such as fractures, are particularly easy to spot, whatever the method of examination. The same is also true for degenerative conditions like osteoarthritis, which seems to have been very widespread and to have affected mainly the spinal column. This complaint was often associated with scoliosis (the lateral curvature of the spine) and seems to have been linked with agricultural work in the fields and with carrying heavy weights.

The detection of such parasitic diseases as bilharzia and filariasis, on the other hand, depends on X-ray analysis, since scientific examinations of the tissues are liable to cause irreversible damage to the mummy.

Tuberculosis and diseases of the heart and blood vessels have been identified, but evidence of cancer is hard to find. This must be due to the fact that cancer frequently attacks the soft organs, which are no longer available for study.

Practically Everyone Was in Poor Health

The village of Duch was occupied between the 1st

The upper jaw of a mummy from Duch, showing damage caused by abscesses.

Statuette of the protective deity Ptah Patek. Note how the dome of the skull and the trunk are fully formed, while the base of the skull and limbs are underdeveloped. This type of dwarfism was fairly common in ancient Egypt.

Opposite below: The mummified head of a seven-year-old girl (right). The presence of the wig in which she was buried (left) pointed to typhoid as the cause of death. Beneath the wig the child's hair had fallen out and was growing back in an irregular fashion— both features of prolonged forms of the illness.

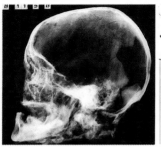

century BC and the 5th century AD. A study of nearly two hundred mummies and skeletons from the necropolis of the village has concluded that almost everyone was suffering from some medical complaint. Spinal osteoarthritis, dislocations, and malnourishment were found to be the most common problems.

Occasionally, clinical observations and X-ray examination have been able to pinpoint the actual cause of death, as in the case of a seven-year-old girl apparently suffering from typhoid, or that of another child who died as a result of a fractured skull. Physical deprivation and hard labor, combined with an almost total lack of medical provision, were the chief causes of the villagers' almost universal poor health.

A photograph and X-ray of the damaged skull of a mummy from Duch with the mummified remains (right) of the brain, found in the skull cavity. The head had become detached from the body (a fairly common occurrence), and in order to hold it in place the embalmer had inserted a palm frond down the spine. In doing so he appears to have shattered the back of the skull.

Scientific Investigation Has Not Destroyed the Mystique Mummies Have

Mummies have always been the object of fascination mixed with fear, partly, no doubt, because by their very

nature they bring us face to face with death and what we might regard as a kind of life after death (however artificial it may be). Another factor is the exciting way in which they telescope time, bringing us in contact with individuals who lived many thousands of years ago— particularly when many of the individuals in question are kings who played such an important role in history as Tuthmosis III and Ramses II.

As the equivalent of ghosts and other potentially maleficent beings, mummies have found their way into the collective unconscious and have created their own film and literary culture. The modern image of the mummy as a baleful creature come to wreak havoc among the living in fulfillment of some ancient curse curiously echoes an obsession of the ancient Egyptians themselves, who believed that the dead could return and take revenge on the living.

Mummification has been practiced in many cultures around the world. The mummy above was found in Peru.

The underground cemetery of the Monastery of the Capuchins in Palermo, Sicily (now a museum), houses thousands of desiccated bodies, dressed in what was once their greatest finery and grouped in corridors (men, women, officials, monks). A bishop (left) presided over the priests' corridor.

Mummification is not the exclusive preserve of the religion of ancient Egypt. In the history of both East and West, there is a longstanding tradition of embalming (or desiccation)—a treatment that has been extended at various times to those living in Sicily, the Aleutian Islands, the Canary Islands, Mexico, and the Andes.

Modern medicine has devised additional ways of stabilizing the body after death, allowing burial to be postponed. One technique uses liquid nitrogen as a medium for freezing the body and preserving it in anticipation of a time when whatever was the cause of death can be cured; at that point the body will be brought back to life. The ancient Egyptians might well have regarded such a process as the ultimate in mummification.

Embalming was practiced by many civilizations, but only the ancient Egyptians truly mastered the art. The Andean mummy (opposite right), the bishop from the monastery in Palermo (opposite left), and the mummies from Guanajuato, Mexico (below), were produced by more or less natural desiccation. Such mummies often look like clothed skeletons. Overleaf: Mourners in the tomb of Ramose.

DOCUMENTS

Funeral Rites

The majority of funerary texts were found in the tombs themselves. They are mainly religious in nature, but they include the odd civil document, such as a bill for a funeral.

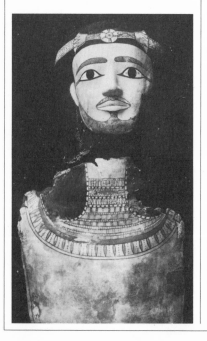

The *Book of the Dead:* The Declaration of Innocence

During the New Kingdom it became customary to place in the tomb, somewhere near the body, a scroll of papyrus containing texts whose purpose was to prepare the dead person for the afterlife. The Book of the Dead, *as these rather stereotyped texts were known, can be traced back directly to the Middle Kingdom Coffin Texts, themselves derived from the earlier Pyramid Texts. The texts were intended as both a guide for the dead person in the journey in the afterlife and a collection of magic formulas designed to ensure safe passage through that other world.*

Chapter 125, which relates to the "Weighing of the Heart" ceremony, is particularly famous. During this ceremony the dead assert their innocence in the presence of Osiris, and if they succeed in passing the test they are said to be "justified."

Homage to thee, O Great God, thou Lord of double Maati, I have come to thee, O my Lord, and I have brought myself hither that I may behold thy beauties. I know thee, and I know thy name, and I know the name[s] of the two and forty gods who exist with thee in this Hall of double Maati, who live as warders of sinners and who feed on their blood on the day when the lives of men are taken into account in the presence of the god Un-nefer.... I have not done evil to mankind. I have not oppressed the members of my family, I have not wrought evil in the place of right and truth. I have not had knowledge of worthless men. I have

Mask and cartonnage of a Middle Kingdom mummy (11th dynasty).

wrought no evil. I have not thought scorn of god. I have not defrauded the oppressed one of his property. I have not done that which is an abomination unto the gods. I have not caused harm to be done to the servant by his chief. I have not caused pain, I have made no man to suffer hunger. I have made no one to weep. I have done no murder. I have not given the order for murder to be done for me. I have not inflicted pain upon mankind. I have not defrauded the temples of their oblations. I have not purloined the cakes of the gods. I have not carried off the cakes offered to the *khus*. I have not committed fornication. I have not polluted myself …nor diminished from the bushel. I have neither added to nor filched away land. I have not encroached upon the fields. I have not added to the weights of the scales. I have not misread the pointer of the scales. I have not carried away the milk from the mouths of children. I have not driven away the cattle which were upon their pastures…. I am pure, I am pure, I am pure, I am pure!…therefore let not evil befall me in this land and in this Hall of the double Maati, because I, even I, know the name[s] of these gods who are therein….

The dead person now addresses the forty-two assessor-gods of Osiris:

Hail, thou crusher of bones who cometh forth from Suten-henen [Heracleopolis], I have not uttered falsehood…

Hail, thou who goest backwards, who comes forth from the city of Bast [Bubastis] I have never pried into matters…

Hail, thou lord of two horns, who cometh forth from Satiu, I have not multiplied my speech overmuch…

E. A. Wallis Budge
The Book of the Dead, 1898

Extract From an Embalming Ritual

The technical and religious aspects of embalming were governed by strict rules set out in great detail in the ritual texts. One of these texts has come down to us in the form of two copies from the Greco-Roman period found in the necropolis at Thebes. The original was undoubtedly much older. Though incomplete, the text covers the various stages of the bandaging process, along with the invocations designed to accompany each of the different stages. The gulf between the real and the ideal— as embodied in this protocol—becomes only too apparent when one comes to study the mummies themselves.

VI
Fitting the fingerstalls to the hands and feet.

Following on from this, fit the golden fingerstalls to his hands and feet. Begin with the ends of the four fingers and finish with the left thumb [?]. Wrap with a long piece of red linen from Sais.

Words to be spoken following these procedures:

Osiris [name of the dead person]!
You have just received your gold fingerstalls and your fingers are pure gold and your nails are electrum! You are touched, in truth, by the emanation of Ra, the divine body of Osiris! Your legs will carry you to the eternal abode, and your hands will carry for you as far

as the place of infinite duration, for you are regenerated by gold and revived by electrum. Your fingers will glitter in the abode of Osiris, in the embalming workshop of Horus himself....

VII
Second unction and wrapping of the head.

Anoint both his head and his mouth, each with oil for "reattaching the head and reattaching the face." Bind with the cloth of Re'-Harakhty of Heliopolis. The cloth of Nekhbet of el-Kab should be placed on top of his head; the cloth of Hathor, lady of Dendera, on his face, and that of Thoth, who separates the Two Combatants, on his ears; the cloth of Nebet-Hetepet on the nape of his neck....

Twenty-two rolls for the right and the left of the face, to be wound at the level of his ears....

Then, following this, bind very carefully with a bandage of two fingers' width....

Words to be spoken following this:

Venerable and Great One, lady of the West, sovereign of the East, come, penetrate to the ears of Osiris [name]!...

Make him see with his eye and hear with his ears; make him breathe with his nose and speak with his mouth; make him use his tongue to argue inside the Douat!

Jean Claude Goyon
Rituels Funéraires de l'Ancienne Egypte
1972

The Harpist's Song

The funerary texts inscribed in New Kingdom tombs often included what has been called the Harpist's Song. With slight variations, the song always treats the same themes, in particular the transitoriness of human life. While not denying the reality of the "second life," it stresses the impossibility of going back and the importance of "living a happy day"—of making the most of this life while waiting to enter the "land that loves silence."

For a generation passes,
and another remains, since the time of
  the ancestors,
those gods who existed aforetime,
who rest in their pyramids,
  and the blessed noble dead likewise,
  buried in their pyramids.
The builder of chapels, their places are
  no more.
What has become of them?
I have heard the words of Imhotep and
  Hordedef,
whose sayings are so told:
What of their places? Their walls have
  fallen;
their places are no more, like those who
  never were.

Harpist performing a lament for a dead person.

None returns from there to tell their
  conditions,
to tell their state, to reassure us,
until we attain the place where they
  have gone.
May you be happy with this,
  forgetfulness giving you benediction.
Follow your heart while you live!
Put myrrh on your head!
Clothe yourself with fine linen!
Anoint yourself with true wonders of
  the divine rite!
Increase your happiness!
Be not weary-hearted! Follow your
  heart and happiness!
Make your things on earth! Do not
  destroy your heart,
until that day of lamentation comes for
  you!
The weary-hearted does not hear their
  lamentation; mourning cannot save a
  man from the tomb-pit.
Make holiday! Do not weary of it!
Look, no one can take his things with
  him.
Look, no one who has gone there
  returns again.

Richard B. Parkinson,
*Voices from Ancient Egypt: An Anthology
of Middle Kingdom Writings,* 1991

A Breakdown of Funeral Expenses

*Papyri from the Greco-Roman period
contain several accounts detailing funeral
expenses. The following text was found
in a village in the Fayuum called
Soknopaiou Nesos. The major costs are
for the fabric for dressing the mummy
and for the funerary mask.*

Pot for embalming oil.

	[drachmas]	[obols]
.....	12 dr	2 ob
Earthenware pot		2 ob
Red paint	4 dr	19 ob
Wax	12 dr	
Myrrh	4 dr	4 ob
Song [dirge?]		4 ob
Tallow		8 ob
Linen clothes	36 dr	16 ob
Mask	64 dr	
Cedar oil	41 dr	
Medicament for linen	4 dr	
Good oil	4 dr	
Turbon's wages	8 dr	
Lamp wicks	24 dr	
Cost of an old tunic		24 ob
Sweet wine		20 ob
Barley	16 dr	
Leaven	4 dr	
Dog	8 dr	
Little mask [?]	14 dr	
2 artabae of loaves	21 dr	
Pine cone		8 ob
Weepers	32 dr	
Carriage by donkey	8 dr	
Chaff [?]		12 ob
TOTAL	440 dr	16 ob

[The total is in fact wrong.]

G. Elliot Smith
and Warren R. Dawson,
Egyptian Mummies, 1924

Mummification According to Herodotus

Toward the middle of the 5th century BC, the Greek historian Herodotus visited Egypt (then a province of the Persian Empire), eager to learn all he could about the country.

Though disparaged in certain quarters ("Herodotus is a liar," claimed one critic), his account of his travels includes some remarkable observations. Much of what Herodotus describes he witnessed with his own eyes; he gathered other information where possible from "the experts." His description of the mummification process is our principal source of information and has been corroborated in large part by modern research.

In this occupation certain persons employ themselves regularly and inherit this as a craft....Then they after they have agreed for a certain price depart out of the way, and the others being left behind in the building embalm according to the best of these ways thus: first with a crooked iron tool they draw out the brain through the nostrils, extracting it partly thus and partly by pouring in drugs; and after this with a sharp stone of Ethiopia they make a cut along the side and take out the whole contents of the belly, and when they have cleared out the cavity and cleansed it with palm wine they cleanse it again with spices pounded up: then they fill the belly with pure myrrh pounded up and with cassia and other spices except frankincense, and sew it together again. Having so done they keep it for embalming covered up in natron for seventy days but for a longer time than this is not permitted to embalm it; and when the seventy days are past, they wash the corpse and roll its whole body up in fine linen cut into bands, smearing these beneath with gum, which the Egyptians use generally instead of glue. Then the kinsfolk receive it from them and have a wooden figure made in the shape of a man, and when they have

Above: A sarcophagus said to have belonged to Alexander. Opposite: A bust of Herodotus.

had this made they enclose the corpse, and having shut it up within, they store it in a sepulchral chamber, setting it to stand upright against the wall. Thus they deal with the corpses which are prepared in the most costly way; but for those who desire the middle way and wish to avoid great cost they prepare the corpse as follows: having filled their syringes with the oil which is got from cedar-wood, with this they forthwith fill the belly of the corpse, and this they do without having either cut it open or taken out the bowels, but they inject the oil by the breech, and, having stopped the drench from returning back they keep it then the appointed number of days for embalming, and on the last of these days they let the cedar oil come out from the belly, which they before put in, and it has such power that it brings out with it the bowels and interior organs of the body dissolved; and the natron dissolves the flesh, so that there is left of the corpse only the skin and the bones. When they have done this they give back the corpse at once in that condition without working upon it any more. The third kind of embalming, by which are prepared the bodies of those who have less means is as follows: they cleanse out the body with a purge and then keep the body for embalming during the seventy days, and at once after that they give it back to the bringers to carry away.

The History of Herodotus, book II, transl. George Campbell Macaulay, 1890

An Unpeaceful End

There have always been looters and collectors eager for whatever riches a tomb might house, and no mummies—illustrious or anonymous—have enjoyed the peace to which they were supposedly entitled.

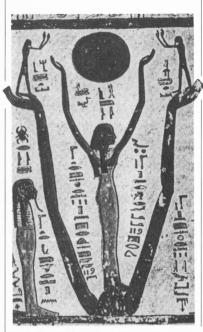

The creation of the new solar disk, in a painting in Ramses VI's burial chamber.

The Pillaging of the Royal Tombs

Under Ramses I and II (19th dynasty), Egypt regained its former glory, but after Ramses III the 20th dynasty witnessed a gradual decline in royal power and a corresponding increase in the power of the priesthood. Emboldened by the political unrest, during Ramses IX's reign, looters extended their activities to include the royal tombs near Thebes. The mayor of Thebes, whose name was Paser, began an investigation, which led to the arrest and trial of several robbers. The following is an extract from the report drawn up by Paser's commission.

The pyramid-tomb of King Sekhemre Shedtaui, son of Re Sobekemsaf. It was found to have been violated by the thieves by tunnelling in the nfrw-chamber of its pyramid from the outer hall of the rock tomb of Nebamun, overseer of the granary of King Menkheperre. The burial-chamber of the king was found empty of its lord and likewise the burial-chamber of the great royal wife, Nubkhaas his consort, the thieves having laid their hands on them. The vizier, the notables and the butlers investigated the matter, and the nature of the attack which the thieves had made on this king and his consort was discovered.

Thomas E. Peet,
The Great Tomb-Robberies of the Twentieth Egyptian Dynasty, 1930

Extract from the robbers' statement:

We went to rob tombs in accordance with our regular habit, we found the pyramid of King Sekhemre-shedtawy, son of Re Sebekemsaf, this being not at all like the pyramids and tombs of the nobles which we habitually went to rob. We took our copper tools and we broke into this pyramid of this king through its innermost part. We found its underground chambers and we took lighted candles in our hands and we went down.

Then we broke through the rubble that we found at the mouth of his recess and found this god lying at the back of his burial-place. And we found the burial-place of Queen Nubkhaas, his queen, situated beside him, it being protected and guarded by plaster and covered with rubble. This we also broke through and found her [resting] there in similar fashion. We opened their sarcophagi and their coffins in which they were, and found the noble mummy of this king equipped with a falchion; a large number of amulets and jewels of gold were upon his neck, and his head-piece of gold was upon him.

The noble mummy of this king was completely bedecked with gold, and his coffins were adorned with gold and silver inside and out and inlaid with all sorts of precious stones. We collected the gold we found on the noble mummy of this god, together with his amulets and jewels which were on his neck and [that on] the coffins in which he was resting, [and we] found the queen in exactly the same state. We collected all that we found upon her likewise and set fire to their coffins. We took their furniture which we found with them consisting of articles of gold, silver and bronze, and divided them among ourselves. And we made into eight parts the gold which we found on these two gods coming from their

mummies, amulets, jewels and coffins and 20 *deben* of gold fell to each of the eight of us, making 160 *deben* of gold, the fragments of furniture not being included. Then we crossed over to Thebes.

In A. J. Spencer
Death in Ancient Egypt, 1982

The Acquisition and Sale of Egyptian Antiquities by a European in the 19th Century

In the 19th century both England and France were engaged in the collection of Egyptian antiquities, which often led to rivalry over the best pieces. For England, consul-general Henry Salt (1780–1827), was aided by Giovanni Belzoni (1778–1823), collector extraordinaire. With Belzoni's help Henry Salt put together three large collections of pieces. The first was bought by the British Museum in London, and the second was acquired by the King of France and is now in the Louvre. The third collection was sold after Salt's death by Sotheby's and again a great deal of it was bought by the British Museum. Salt's interpreter and agent was Giovanni d'Athanasi, who wrote his memoirs of his experiences in Egypt.

In the excavations at Abydos we do not find any great variety of mummies—they are chiefly of one kind, and enclosed in wooden cases. The tombs in the plain are all lined with a coating of brick-work, arched at the top and covered with plaister [sic], a precaution rendered indispensable by reason of the friable nature of the sandy rock which predominates in the neighbourhood. On the four walls of the principal chamber are compartments expressly provided for the reception of the usual tablets and statues, and on the pavement are sarcophagi of calcareous stone of ordinary workmanship. These chambers do not contain more than two or three of these sarcophagi....The tablets and idols, and other objects found with the mummies in these tombs are all of the same style. Those who ransacked the tombs in search of gold and silver, have succeeded so well in obtaining access even to the uttermost chambers, that I have not had the good fortune to find a single tomb in these parts which had not been opened before, and of course those that I did enter were knocked about and injured by those who had preceded me.

During the whole of my sojourn in Abydos I only found two mummies in an untouched and perfect state, which were contained in cases of very ordinary make. These two cases are now in London, one of them belonging, I believe, to Mr. Sams, who bought it of me with some other articles of antiquity when he was in Egypt.

A circumstance which I regard as peculiarly interesting with respect to the tombs at Abydos is that all the mummies are embalmed after the same manner, and with one kind of balm, instead of different materials as is the case at Thebes. At Abydos the bodies are universally found preserved with the black balm which I have already mentioned; at least in the course of all our excavations we did not find one of any other kind. This would lead one to believe that the black embalment was the first in point of antiquity of all that the ancients adopted. Mr. Salt's opinion, which is also concurred in by Mr. Wilkinson, was that the city of Abydos was more ancient than Thebes.

To his account of his adventures in Egypt, Athanasi added a catalogue of the sale of Salt's third collection, with a short introduction. A total of 1270 lots, of many different kinds of objects, made up the sale. The collection brought a grand total of £7,168 18s 6d.

Three Collections of Egyptian Antiquities were formed by the late Mr. Salt during his residence, as Consul-General in Egypt. On his arrival in that country in the year 1816, he found that Monsieur Drovetti, formerly the French consul, was in Upper Egypt, busily employed in buying up every thing that might add to the Collection of Antiquities which he had been several years in forming, with the view of disposing of them to the French Government.

The following is Athanasi's detailed description of one particular lot (number 150) in the sale:

The Mummy of a Female of high quality, 5 feet 4 in. high, with its case, highly painted and ornamented...£105.

The mask of this Mummy, which is highly ornamented, presents us with a beautiful specimen of that art and elegance oftentimes so admirably displayed by the Ancient Egyptians in their delineation of the human countenance.

The arms are folded across the body, and on the fingers of the left hand are nine cornelian and other rings, those of the right having thereon three. The whole of the upper part of the body and head was ornamented with wreaths of the sun flower, which were, according to the custom, only placed on the mummified bodies of those persons that were unmarried. These ornaments fell to pieces soon after the opening of the case.

In front of the body are attached two tablets, the first in silver and gold work, representing a jackal on a pedestal; the other, of similar work having in the centre a Scarabeus of stone...with seven lines of hieroglyphics, on either side of a priest with uplifted hands, and on the top the emblem of the soul with extended wings. In the inside of the case is the platted [*sic*] hair of the deceased enveloped in cloth, and also a small idol, in the form of a mummy, with silver work.

This is one of the most curious and interesting Mummies extant, and doubtless contains all the numerous rings as represented on the fingers, and other beautiful ornaments.

Giovanni d'Athanasi,
A Brief Account of the Researches and Discoveries in Upper Egypt, Made under the Direction of Henry Salt, Esq.,
1836

In the 19th century European tourists, guided by Egyptians, visited and rummaged through ancient tombs.

Two Sensational Discoveries

The systematic exploration of Egypt during the last century led to the discovery of a number of royal tombs. Illustrious pharaohs saw the light of day once more, and mummies became an important focus of research.

The Cache at Deir el-Bahari

In 1875 the antiquities market in Luxor began selling objects clearly originating from royal tombs. Archaeologists took note, and in 1881 Gaston Maspero, newly appointed director of the Antiquities Service, decided to look into it. Suspicion soon fell on a family living in the village of Gourna, the Abd el-Rassul brothers. Under insistent questioning one of the brothers finally broke his silence and revealed the existence of a hiding place stashed full of mummies.

On Wednesday [5 July] Mohammed Ahmed Abd el-Rassul took Emil Brugsch and Ahmed Effendi Kamal to the place where the burial vault was located. The Egyptian engineer originally responsible for tunneling the vault had designed it with the utmost skill: No hiding place was ever better concealed.

At the bottom of the shaft, a corridor 55 feet wide and 31 feet high was tunneled in the west wall. After about 24 feet the corridor turns sharply to the north and continues in that direction for approximately 200 feet, though its dimensions vary: At certain points it is as much as 6 feet wide, at others only about 4 feet. About halfway along, five or six roughly hewn steps mark a drop in the level of the floor and on the right-hand side an unfinished niche of sorts shows that another change in direction had originally been planned. The gallery finally opens into a kind of irregular oblong chamber, about 250 feet long.

The first thing Emil Brugsch saw when he arrived at the bottom of the

Tutankhamun's tomb contained many treasures, including these alabaster vases.

shaft was a white and yellow coffin bearing the name Nibsonu. The coffin was in the corridor, about 2 feet from the entrance. A little further on was a coffin whose shape recalled the style of the 17th dynasty; next to it lay the coffin of Queen Tiuhathor Honttoui; next to that, Seti I's. Scattered all over the floor alongside the coffins were boxes of funerary statuettes, Canopic jars, bronze libation vases, and, right at the back, in the angle made by the corridor as it turns north, Queen Isimkheb's funeral tent, folded and crumpled as if it were an object of no value—no doubt carelessly thrown in the corner by a priest in a hurry to leave. The main corridor was equally cluttered and chaotic, and we had to crawl along it without knowing where we were putting our hands and feet. The coffins and the mummies, glimpsed in the candlelight, bore historic names: among them, Amenophis I and Tuthmos [Tuthmosis] II (in the niche by the stairs), Ahmose [Amosis] I and his son Siamun, Soqnunri [Seqenenre], Queen Ahhotpu [Aahotep] and Ahmose Nofritari [Ahmose Nefertari]. The end chamber was the most jumbled of all, but here the style was predominantly that of the 20th dynasty, recognizable at a glance. Mohammed Ahmed Abd el-Rassul's story, which had seemed fanciful at first, scarcely did justice to the truth: where I had expected to meet one or two petty kings, the Arabs had uncovered a whole vault full of kings. And what kings! Perhaps the most famous in the history of Egypt— Thutmos [Tuthmosis] III and Seti I, Ahmose [Amosis] the Liberator and Ramses II the Conqueror. Emil Brugsch thought he must be dreaming,

The mummy of Seti I, discovered in the royal cache at Deir el-Bahari.

stumbling unexpectedly into such company, and when I see, and touch, the bodies of so many illustrious persons we never imagined could be more than names to us, like him I still find it hard to believe that I am not dreaming.

Two hours sufficed for this initial examination, then the removal work began. The mudir's men swiftly assembled three hundred Arabs and these men set to work.... Mohammed went down the shaft and organized the removal procedure from there, while Emil Brugsch and Ahmed Effendi Kamal took charge of the objects as they came to the surface, transported them to the foot of the hill and lay them alongside one another, keeping a close eye on everything as they did so. Emptying the tomb took forty-eight hours of hard labor, but the job was only half done then. We still had to take the goods across the Theban plain and over the river to Luxor. Some of the coffins required twelve to sixteen men to lift them, and even then it was a tremendous struggle, and it took the men seven or eight hours to get from the mountain to the river. It is not hard to imagine what such a journey was like in the dust and the July heat. Finally, on the evening of the 11th, the mummies and the coffins were all in Luxor, duly wrapped in cloth and matting. Three days later the museum's steamer arrived and as soon as it was loaded left again for Bulaq with its cargo of kings. Then a strange thing happened. From Luxor to Kuft, on either bank of the Nile, disheveled peasant women followed the boat howling like animals, and the men fired shots in the way that they do at a funeral.

Gaston Maspero
La Trouvaille de Deir el-Bahari
1881

The Opening of Tutankhamun's Sarcophagus

On 4 November 1922, after several years spent scouring the Valley of the Kings, Howard Carter discovered the tomb of Tutankhamun, but the long and painstaking process of opening the sarcophagus and the three coffins that lay inside it began on 10 October 1925.

This great gilded wooden coffin, 7 feet 4 in. in length, anthropoid in shape, wearing the Khat head-dress, with face and hands in heavier sheet-gold, is of Rishi type [named for the decoration imitating feathered wings]....

It was a moment as anxious as exciting. The lid came up fairly readily, revealing a second magnificent anthropoid coffin, covered with a thin gossamer linen sheet, darkened and much decayed. Upon this linen shroud were lying floral garlands, composed of olive and willow leaves, petals of the blue lotus and cornflowers, whilst a small wreath of similar kind had been placed, also over the shroud, on the emblems of the forehead. Underneath this covering, in places, glimpses could be obtained of rich multi-coloured glass decoration encrusted upon the fine gold-work of the coffin....

Further records having been taken, I was then able to remove the chaplet and garlands, and roll back the covering shroud. It was one more exciting moment. We could now gaze, with admiring eyes, upon the finest example of the ancient coffin-maker's art ever yet seen—Osiride, again in form, but most delicate in conception, and very beautiful in line....

This revealed a third coffin which, like its predecessors, was Osiride in form, but the main details and the workmanship were hidden by a close-fitting reddish-coloured linen shroud. The burnished gold face was bare; placed over the neck and breast was an elaborate bead and floral collarette, sewn upon a backing of papyrus, and tucked immediately above the Nemes head-dress was a linen napkin.

Mr. Burton at once made his photographic records. I then removed the floral collarette and linen coverings. An astounding fact was disclosed. This third coffin, 6 feet 1¾ of an inch in length, was made of solid gold!...

But the ultimate details of the ornamentation were hidden by a black lustrous coating due to liquid unguents that had evidently been profusely poured over the coffin....The lid was raised by its golden handles and the mummy of the king disclosed....

Before us, occupying the whole of the interior of the golden coffin, was an impressive, neat and carefully made mummy, over which had been poured anointing unguents as in the case of the outside of its coffin—again in great quantity—consolidated and blackened by age. In contradistinction to the general dark and sombre effect, due to these unguents, was a brilliant, one might say magnificent, burnished gold mask or similitude of the king, covering his head and shoulders, which, like the feet, had been intentionally avoided when using the unguents. The mummy was fashioned to symbolize Osiris. The beaten gold mask, a beautiful and unique specimen of ancient portraiture, bears a sad but calm expression suggestive of youth overtaken prematurely by death.... The burnished gold hands, crossed over the breast, separate from the mask, were sewn to the material of the linen wrappings, and grasped the flagellum

and crozier—the emblems of Osiris....

Though the attributes upon this mummy are those of the gods, the likeness is certainly that of Tut.ankh.Amen, comely and placid, with the features recognizable on all his statues and coffins....

When the detailed photographic records were made by Mr. Burton, we were better able to make a closer examination of the actual state of things, and the preservation of the mummy. The greater part of the flagellum and crozier was completely decomposed, and had already fallen to dust; the threads that once held the hands and trappings in place upon the outer linen covering were decayed, and in consequence the various sections fell apart at the slightest touch.... The farther we proceeded the more evident it became that the covering wrapping and the mummy were in a parlous state. They were completely carbonized by the action that had been set up by the fatty acids of the unguents with which they had been saturated.

Howard Carter
The Tomb of Tut.ankh.Amen
vol. 2, 1927

Howard Carter removing the funeral couch from Tutankhamun's tomb.

Looking into Mummies

Wilhelm Conrad Röntgen's discovery of X-rays in 1895 provided a way of studying mummies without damaging them. The only problem was logistical: How to bring mummy, radiologist, and equipment together in one place.

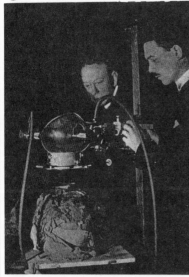

Je sais tout
La Grande Revue de
Vulgarisation Scientifique

X-raying a Mummy

In 1926 two journalists from the popular French science magazine Je Sais Tout *expressed their surprise that the mummy of Tutankhamun, whose tomb had been discovered four years earlier, had not been X-rayed. (It was, in fact, but much later.) The journalists decided to experiment. They approached the Musée Guimet in Lyons, where a Professor Moret directed them to the mummy of a female musician.*

There was one preliminary test which we had to do, upon which the success or failure of our entire experiment could be said to depend: A fluoroscopy. In other words, before we could hope to obtain a sensitive plate printed with the X-ray image, it was essential to ascertain that the rays could produce an image on a simple fluorescent screen....

Despite the thickness of the table and the web of bandages, the beam of strange rays penetrated through to the fluorescent plate, and on the lighted background of the plate we saw two long dark streaks appear, then two shorter ones—the mummy's tibias and fibias!...

It took us several hours, and we had to proceed by trial and error, dealing with each problem as it occurred. The first thing to understand is that our X-ray was completed in sections: The light source was directed from above this time, while we slid the sensitive plates under each of the different parts of the body in turn—head, neck, trunk, pelvis, etc. But what a lot of little problems kept cropping up!...

The X-rays were interpreted by the joint efforts of a surgeon, Professor G. Lardennois, and an Egyptologist, Professor Moret—evidence of the dual interest, anthropological and

Egyptological, of this type of research....

"I don't know how to congratulate you enough on your bizarre initiative," this eminent surgeon said to us. "There is certainly a great deal to be learned from studies of this kind. Your X-ray provides all sorts of useful anthropological information. The forehead is wide and the head well formed, showing that your Egyptian was undoubtedly an intelligent woman. Her general skeletal makeup—which has no flaws or fractures that I can identify—is that of a healthy, and I would go so far as to say, athletic, individual.

"There is one striking thing, however, and that is the abnormal distension of the thorax.... I suspect this must be because the embalmers stuffed the chest cavity, and quite energetically, too...."

M. Moret, professor at the Collège de France, had been particularly recommended to us for his knowledge of Egyptology....

Professor Moret explained that during mummification the cavities of the body—first emptied of the viscera—were indeed stuffed very vigorously....

"The X-rays produced by your machine were able to penetrate most areas of the body, but in the trunk they struck a compact mass, which shows up in black on your photograph. What is this mass—this thick stuffing—you may wonder. It is almost certainly a mixture of earth, resin, and aromatic plants. It may also be that the embalmers replaced the dead woman's viscera....

"What a lot of interesting things your X-ray photograph shows!... Yes, the archaeologist gains new insights and clarification from your X-ray, and it is to be hoped that closer and closer links will be established between the different

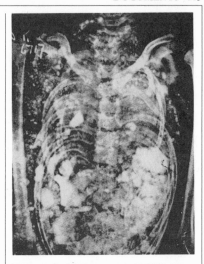

X-ray of a child's mummy by P. H. K. Gray. The embalmers stuffed the abdomen with rubble to prevent the body from sagging.

sciences—however dissimilar their objectives may appear—to the advantage of each."

C. Leleux and M. Gouineau
Je Sais Tout
March 1926 and April 1926

The Largest Series of Mummies X-rayed

During the 1960s P. H. K. Gray X-rayed 133 Egyptian mummies in a number of European museums. In a brief review of all such studies carried out to that point, Gray expresses surprise that X-raying was still a relatively rare approach, even where detailed work was being done. His studies remain the most extensive of their kind to this day.

Since radiography has no deleterious effect on a wrapped mummy, and in view of the paucity of reports on the radiologic examination of mummies, it was thought worthwhile to obtain permission to radiograph the specimens in the museums of Great Britain and other European countries. The objectives were to determine the presence or absence of human bones; to determine the age and the sex of the person; to correlate the radiographic findings with the various embalming technics; to demonstrate amulets within the wrappings; and to demonstrate pathological changes....

Gray elaborates on the X-ray method.

Archaeology: determination of the presence or absence of human bones. The large museums of Great Britain and other European countries contain many mummies purchased in Egypt by

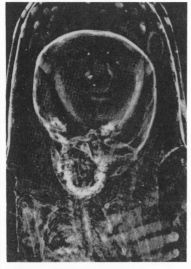

X-ray of a child's skull by Gray superimposed on the mummy's mask.

early nineteenth-century explorers and travellers. The native dealers were quick to realise that a good profit could be made from the sale of "souvenirs" and mummies—forgeries were by no means uncommon. In 1837, [C. Rochfort] Scott wrote: "For the eagerness with which every sort of trash is purchased makes the trade a very profitable concern, and opens a wide door for fraud by the encouragement it gives to the manufacture of mummies." This study has confirmed Scott's statement. On many an occasion, a traveller had been sold not a mummy, but a modern fake.

Determination of age and sex. A coffin can usually be dated by its orthography and style, but it cannot be assumed that the coffin contains its original inhabitant. For example, a coffin bearing the names and the titles of a man may contain the mummy of a woman, and vice versa.

In one case a specimen appeared to be the unwrapped mummy of a woman 75 years old. Radiography, however, showed it to be that of a girl about 17 years old.

Correlation of radiographic findings with known embalming technics. It has been possible to correlate radiographic findings with known embalming technics, especially in mummies of the Twenty-first Dynasty, wherein the salient features are visceral packs within the body cavity, artificial eyes, and subcutaneous plumping of the body.

Demonstration of amulets. Being radiopaque, the amulets can be detected easily, and when desirable can be and have been localised with ease and removed through small incisions in the wrappings.

Palaeopathology. Moodie pointed out, "Roentgenology supplements all other methods of learning of physical troubles in early times." It was originally thought that only bony lesions would be found. Such, however, was not the case.

Osteoarthritis. Osteoarthritis of the vertical column was common.

Lines of arrested growth. These were present in a little over 30 percent of the 133 mummies examined.

Fractures. Numerous fractures and dislocations were found, especially in late-period mummies, but they were nearly all postmortem.

Other bony features. The state of the feet indicates that restrictive footwear was not worn.

Dental condition. Dental disease and attrition were found to be very common.

Lesions of soft tissue. Among the 27 mummies in the museum at Leiden, 20 are those of adults. In at least four of these, there was extensive calcification of the arteries of the legs.

Gallstones were almost certainly present in one of the 133 mummies and were possibly present in another.

Important diseases not found. No evidence of the following important diseases was found in the skeletons of the mummies:…malignant neoplasia, tuberculosis, syphilis, leprosy or rickets.

P. H. K. Gray,
"Radiography of Ancient Egyptian Mummies," *Medical Radiography and Photography*, vol. 43, no.2, 1967

Ramses II in Paris

In 1975, following an agreement between the French and Egyptian governments, the mummy of Ramses was taken to Paris for treatment.

In 1912 X-rays had shown that the mummy was deteriorating, and it needed urgent attention. X-rays were to reveal not only a number of pathological changes, but also the presence of artifacts resulting from embalming. They also led to the conclusion that Ramses II had suffered a fracture to the cervical spine during embalming, at the precise moment when the resin was being poured into his cranial cavity.

From the minute he arrived in Paris, scientists worked assiduously to save Ramses. The first task was to determine the exact cause of his illness. Among the remains of the linen wrappings, some samples of minute fragments from the mummy's chest and some fallen hairs were collected and immediately analyzed.… Was it bacteria? Fungus? Insects? the experts all brought their most sophisticated microscopes to bear on the problem.… It was Dr. Jean Mouchacca, a cryptogram specialist at the Musée d'Histoire Naturelle, who succeeded in identifying the destructive organism: a fungus with the preposterous name of *Daedalea biennis Fries*.…

The in-depth study of Ramses' skeleton, the walls of his femoral arteries, his teeth, and his whole mummified body, proved highly revealing. It appears that Ramses suffered from a slight limp and a stiffening of the spinal column, and that his head was inclined too far forward in relation to his spine. When he was buried, the embalmers straightened his head, causing visible fracturing to the front and back of his neck. The pharaoh had numerous abscesses in his teeth, and all the evidence suggests that he died as a result of a general infection.

Uncovering the cause of Ramses' illness was one thing; saving him was quite another. Lionel Balout and Colette Roubet knew this only too well. It was time to act and to arrest the problem using all the means that modern technology placed at their disposal. Chemotherapy, and any kind of treatment using heat or cold, were quickly dismissed as possibilities. The reason for this was that no one knew how the resins and gums employed during the embalming process would react to such treatments: there were too many imponderables. Only one solution remained: to subject Ramses II to radiation treatment. It was a difficult decision for which to take sole responsibility. If the pharaoh were even the slightest bit damaged, diplomatic relations with the Egyptians would no doubt suffer.

From the start of the operation the mummy was handled with the utmost care and remained under the watchful eye of Dr. Sawki Nakhla, Egypt's official representative. The base of the oak coffin, the vehicle in which the king had been traveling, was cut away so that a sheet of altuglas could be slid under the body and this then transferred to an operating table. The head and torso were propped up with small cushions to avoid putting any strain on the skeleton, and the body was exposed only while the scientists were working on it, and then never for more than three hours at a stretch....

The key word, therefore, was caution. The scientists had no option but to take action, however. Jean Mouchacca's diagnosis was explicit: if they failed to eradicate the fungus, by the end of the century Ramses II's mummy would be entirely eaten up by it. Balout alone was in a position to decide on the form of treatment that should be applied. His verdict: radiation....

Ramses II was first restored, with infinite care, by the specialists at the Musée de l'Homme, then draped in a piece of antique linen cloth courtesy of the Louvre and placed in his cedarwood coffin. He had been reborn a second time and recovered all his former radiance. The doctors who tended him merely played the same part that the priests had played before them. Respecting ancient tradition, they had given Ramses' spirit the dwelling it desired: a perfect body. And from within this frail frame the king now gazes down on the river of life.

Sygma

The Mummies from Duch

Mummies in museums are often of unknown provenance and have essentially been selected for their careful workmanship and good condition. Studying mummies on site is a better way of sampling a population as a whole.

In 1976 Serge Sauneron, director of the Institut Français d'Archéologie Orientale in Cairo, obtained a concession to carry out excavations at Duch, a village in the extreme south of the Kharga oasis, in the Libyan desert. The site had been known since the beginning of the 19th century, but it had never been investigated. And yet it had much to commend it: a stone temple, almost intact, surrounded by a huge unfired brick enclosure, a temple built of unfired brick, the remains of a village whose inhabitants must have numbered around five thousand at the height of its prosperity, and a vast necropolis. The site is known to have been occupied between the 1st century BC and the beginning of the 5th century AD, roughly corresponding to Roman domination of Egypt. Although this is a very late period in ancient Egyptian history, cultural and religious traditions had persisted to a remarkable degree in this small community far removed from the centers of power.

The excavations (still in progress) of the necropolis have uncovered more than seven hundred bodies in either a mummified or a skeletal state. Careful examination of the skeletons has revealed that as a general rule these too bear traces of mummification. The poor condition of these human remains is due to systematic pillaging and—since the necropolis lies right along the fields—flooding from irrigation canals. The skeletons have been studied according to classical osteometric methods, but the presence of a fair number of mummies in a satisfactory condition led to the idea of carrying out radiological studies on site. By looking in this way at a homogeneous series (the first time this had occurred) it was possible to establish a cross-section of an entire population.

The complete X-ray process had thus to be carried out in a desert location with no electricity or running water, a feat achieved by using a traditional portable machine connected up to the site generator. The developing lab posed more of a problem, but the final results were comparable to negatives produced by standard procedures.

Most of the mummies have been stripped of their bandages and ornaments and many were encrusted with sand and required careful cleaning to prevent artifacts appearing on the X-rays. The clean-up operation was followed by a clinical description, and a series of photographs was taken to show comparative measurements. Then the X-rays were taken—at least eight negatives in each case to cover all the different parts of the body, with particular attention to the skull, and additional negatives for any area that seems of particular interest.... In some cases samples of hair, nails, skin, resin, and embalming products were taken for analysis. When all these various procedures were completed, the mummies, duly labeled, are placed in tombs that were selected for their security and ease of access.

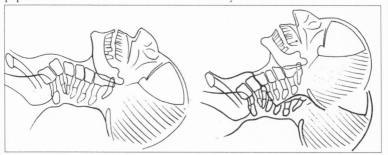

Drawings by Roger Lichtenberg showing the position of Ramses' head before the cervical fracture (top right) and after it (left and bottom right).

The ruins of Duch (above) and some of the seven hundred mummies exhumed there (right).

Results

Our findings show that at Duch we are dealing with a population of Mediterranean type, of slim build and average height (men 1.65 m, women 1.55 m), pale skinned...almost identical in features to the populations of the Nile valley.

Pathological evidence is fairly extensive. In several cases there is evidence of a fatal fracture resulting from trauma: In one case, for example, an old woman died from a fracture to the thighbone; in another, a child died as a result of a fractured skull. Of thirty-eight adults X-rayed, 74 percent were suffering from osteoarthritis of the spinal column —an unusually high percentage probably attributable to manual labor—and an additional 84 percent were suffering from scoliosis. Striae relating to arrested growth were observed in almost two-thirds of the cases (practically double Gray's figure), indicating fairly frequent periods of food shortage. Parasitic illnesses still encountered in Egypt today, such as filariasis and in particular bilharzia, were also identified. But despite the overall state of health of the population, which can only be described as poor, the average lifespan (not taking into account perinatal mortality, which must have been very high) was thirty-eight. Mummification appears to have been virtually universal. Mummies represent about two-fifths of the total human remains, but artifacts characteristic of mummification are indicated for the majority of skeletons. Deterioration was due to the poor

conditions in which the mummies were conserved, and, contrary to popular opinion, the quality of the mummification itself was good. Although abdominal evisceration was rare, removal of the brain was very common, occurring in thirty-three out of fifty-one skulls studied, in other words 65 percent of cases. Differences in the construction of the mummies show that Herodotus's description of the different categories of treatment, from the most rudimentary to the most elaborate, continued to hold good even at this late date. The most elaborate treatment involved gilding the body and in particular the face.

The study of mummies thus supplements that of funerary goods as a means of gauging the relative wealth of different tombs. It also provides evidence for the existence of social differentiation within a population that has otherwise supplied us with scant written information.

Françoise Dunand and
Roger Lichtenberg,
1991

Chronology

before 3100 BC	Predynastic period
c. 3100–2890 BC	Archaic period 1st–2nd dynasties
c. 2686–2181 BC	Old Kingdom 3rd–6th dynasties
2181–2040 BC	1st Intermediate period 7th–11th dynasties
2040–1786 BC	Middle Kingdom end 11th–12th dynasties
1786–1550 BC	2nd Intermediate period 13th–17th dynasties
1550–1085 BC	New Kingdom 18th–20th dynasties
1085–712 BC	3rd Intermediate period 21st–24th dynasties
712–404 BC	Ethiopian and Sais Renaissance 25th–27th dynasties
404–343 BC	Last Egyptian dynasties 28th–30th dynasties
343–332 BC	Second era of Persian rule
322 BC–AD 395	Greco-Roman period

MAP 121

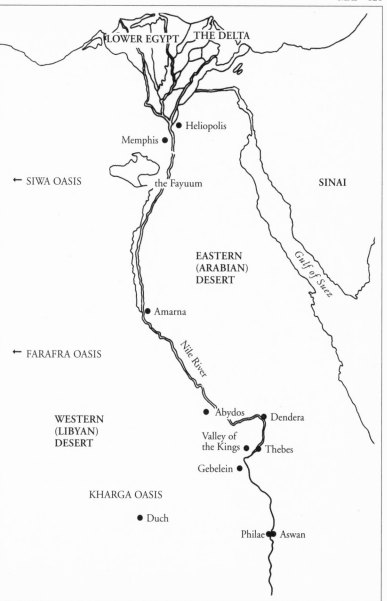

LOWER EGYPT THE DELTA

Heliopolis

Memphis

SIWA OASIS →

the Fayuum

SINAI

EASTERN
(ARABIAN)
DESERT

Gulf of Suez

Amarna

FARAFRA OASIS →

Nile River

Abydos

Dendera

WESTERN
(LIBYAN)
DESERT

Valley of
the Kings

Thebes

Gebelein

KHARGA OASIS

Duch

Philae Aswan

Further Reading

Adams, Barbara, *Egyptian Mummies,* Shire Publications, Princes Risborough, Aylesbury, Bucks, UK, 1984

Aldred, Cyril, *Egypt to the End of the Old Kingdom,* Thames and Hudson, London, 1965

———, *Egyptian Art in the Days of the Pharaohs 3100–320 B.C.,* Thames and Hudson, London, 1980

———, *The Egyptians,* Thames and Hudson, London, 1987

Andrews, Carol, *Egyptian Mummies,* Harvard University Press, Cambridge, Massachusetts, 1984

———, *Ancient Egyptian Jewelry,* Abrams, New York, 1991

Andrews, Carol, ed., *The Ancient Egyptian Book of the Dead,* transl. Raymond O. Faulkner, British Museum Publications, London, 1985

d'Athanasi, Giovanni, *A Brief Account of the Researches and Discoveries in Upper Egypt, Made Under the Direction of Henry Salt, Esq,* John Hearne, London, 1836

Belzoni, Giovanni, *Narrative of the Operations and Recent Discoveries within the Pyramids, Temples, Tombs and Excavations in Egypt and Nubia,* repr. of the 1820 original, Gregg International Publishing

British Museum Department of Egyptian Antiquities, *Catalogue of Egyptian Antiquities in the British Museum,* British Museum, London, 1968

Budge, E. A. Wallis, *The Book of the Dead,* Kegan Paul & Co., London, 1898

———, *The Mummy,* Causeway Books, New York, 1974

Carter, Howard, *The Tomb of Tut.ankh.Amen,* 1927

Clayton, Peter A., *The Rediscovery of Ancient Egypt: Artists and Travellers in the 19th Century,* Thames and Hudson, London, 1982

Cockburn, Aidan, and Eve Cockburn, eds., *Mummies, Disease, and Ancient Cultures,* Cambridge University Press, New York, 1980

David, A. Rosalie, *The Ancient Egyptians: Religious Beliefs and Practices,* Routledge & Kegan Paul, Boston, 1982

David, Rosalie, ed., *Mysteries of the Mummies: The Story of the Manchester University Investigation,* Cassell, London, 1978

Dawson, Warren R., and Eric P. Uphill, *Who Was Who in Egyptology,* 2nd revised ed., Egypt Exploration Society, London, 1972

El Mahdy, Christine, *Mummies, Myth and Magic in Ancient Egypt,* Thames and Hudson, London, 1989

Goyon, Jean-Claude, *Rituels Funeraires de l'Ancienne Egypte,* Editions du Cerf, Paris, 1972

Gray, P. H. K., "Radiography of Ancient Egyptian Mummies," *Medical Radiography and Photography,* vol. 43, no. 2, Rochester, New York, 1967

Hamilton-Paterson, James, and Carol Andrews, *Mummies: Death and Life in Ancient Egypt,* Collins/British Museum Publications, London, 1978

Harris, James E., and Edward F. Wente, eds., *An X-ray Atlas of the Royal Mummies,* University of Chicago Press, Chicago, 1980

Hayes, William C., *The Scepter of Egypt,* 2 vols., Abrams, New York, 1959

Herodotus, *The History of Herodotus,* transl. G. C. Macaulay, 1890

James, T. G. H., *Ancient Egypt: The Land and Its Legacy,* British Museum Publications, London, 1988

Maspero, Gaston, *La Trouvaille de Deir el-Bahari,* Cairo, 1881

Montet, Pierre, *Eternal Egypt,* transl. Doreen Weightman, New American Library, New York, 1964

Parkinson, Richard B., *Voices from Ancient Egypt: An Anthology of Middle Kingdom Writings,* British Museum Press, London, 1991

Peet, Thomas E., *The Great Tomb Robberies of the Twentieth Egyptian Dynasty,* Clarendon Press, Oxford, England, 1930

Smith, G. Elliot, and Warren R. Dawson, *Egyptian Mummies,* Kegan Paul International, New York, repr. 1991

Spencer, A. J., *Death in Ancient Egypt,* Penguin Books, New York, 1982

Taylor, John H., *Egyptian Coffins,* Shire Publications, Princes Risborough, Aylesbury, Bucks, UK, 1989

Vercoutter, Jean, *The Search for Ancient Egypt,* Abrams, New York, 1992

List of Illustrations

Index

Acknowledgments

The authors wish to thank Jean-Louis de Cenival (head curator) and Marie-France Aubert (curator) of the Egyptian antiquities department at the Louvre; the Institut Français d'Archéologie Orientale team; and Alain Leclerc, photographer with the IFAO. The publishers wish to thank for their kind help Jean-Louis de Cenival, head curator of the Egyptian antiquities department at the Louvre; Luc Limme, curator of Egyptian antiquities at the Musée Royal in Brussels; Marie-Françoise Audouard at Editions du Chêne; and Roland Mourer, curator at the Musée Guimet d'Histoire Naturelle in Lyons

Photograph Credits

ACL, Brussels 37r. All rights reserved: spine, 12, 13, 15a, 21a, 21b, 22a, 23, 34a, 41, 42a, 56, 58a, 58–9, 59a, 59b, 61al, 70, 70–1, 72r, 79, 80l, 80r, 81, 86a, 91r, 92b, 94l, 96, 97, 100, 102, 104, 108, 109, 112, 113, 114, 117. Bibliothèque Nationale, Paris 14, 17, 18–9, 32–3, 48–9, 52al, 63, 69a, 73, 74b, 75a, 77, 78al, 103. Boston Museum of Fine Arts 98. British Museum, London 11, 28, 29a, 34–5, 47a, 47b, 50a, 68l. Dagli Orti, Paris 60a. Françoise Dunand 45r. Edimedia, Paris 33. Electa, Milan 29b, 54–5. FMR/Franco Lovera 43a. J. L. Heim 92a, 93bl. IFAO/Alain Leclerc, Paris 74a. J. Liepe, Berlin 43r, 44b, 46b, 50b, 51r, 52b, 54–5, 62ar, 68r. Roger Lichtenberg 1–9, 36r, 76, 82a, 82b, 86b, 87a, 87b, 89, 90, 91l, 93a, 93br, 118, 118–9. Musée de l'Homme, Paris 94r. Musée Guimet d'Histoire Naturelle, Lyons 27, 29c, 32, 35, 51l, 52ar, 53, 54–5. Pelizaeus Museum, Hildesheim 26, 38r, 38b, 88–9. Réunion des Musées Nationaux, Paris: front cover, back cover, 15b, 16, 22b, 30, 30–1, 34c, 36l, 37l, 38–9, 39, 40, 42–3, 44a, 45l, 46a, 54–5, 57, 60b, 61ar, 61b, 62al, 62b, 64, 64–5, 65a, 66, 67l, 67r, 68–9, 101. Manchester Museum 20–1. Roger-Viollet, Paris 31, 72l, 78ar, 78–9, 95, 107, 111. Stierlin/Artephot, Paris 24a, 24b, 24–5, 25. Sygma, Paris 83, 84–5

Text Credits

Grateful acknowledgment is made for use of material from the following: *Voices from Ancient Egypt* by R. B. Parkinson, published by the British Museum Press, 1991 (pp. 100–1); *Egyptian Mummies* by G. Elliot Smith and Warren R. Dawson, courtesy of Kegan Paul International, London and New York (p. 101); *Death in Ancient Egypt* by A. J. Spencer, published by Penguin Books, 1982 (pp. 104–5); reprinted courtesy Eastman Kodak Company (pp. 113–5)

Françoise Dunand is professor of the history of religion at the
University of Strasbourg-II in France. A former member
of the Institut Français d'Archéologie Orientale in Cairo,
she has published a number of books and articles on late
Egyptian religious beliefs and practices. Since 1983 she
has directed IFAO archaeological excavations at the
necropolis at Duch.

Roger Lichtenberg is a medical doctor and director of the
radiology unit at the Institut Arthur-Vernes in Paris. He was a
member of the team that examined the mummy of Ramses II
in Paris in 1976 and has written a number of articles on
clinical radiology and the study of mummies. Since 1982 he
has been in charge of X-raying and conducting
anthropological and palaeopathological studies on the
mummies of Duch.

*To all our colleagues on the Duch excavations and to the
Egyptian workers who helped us in our explorations*

Translated from the French by Ruth Sharman

Editor: Sharon AvRutick
Typographic Designer: Elissa Ichiyasu
Design Assistant: Miko McGinty
Text Permissions: Neil Ryder Hoos

Library of Congress Catalog Card Number: 94–70538

ISBN 0–8109–2886–8

Copyright © 1991 Gallimard

English translation copyright © 1994 Harry N. Abrams, Inc., New York,
and Thames and Hudson Ltd., London

Published in 1994 by Harry N. Abrams, Inc., New York

Printed and bound in Italy by Editoriale Libraria, Trieste